Keeping Your Cool
While Sharing Your Faith

Keeping Your Cool While Sharing Your Faith

by Greg Johnson
& Susie Shellenberger

Tyndale House Publishers, Inc.
WHEATON, ILLINOIS

Unless otherwise indicated, Scripture quotations are from the *Holy Bible,* New International Version. Copyright © 1973, 1978, 1984 International Bible Society. Used by permission of Zondervan Publishing House. All rights reserved. The *"NIV"* and *"New International Version"* trademarks are registered in the United States Patent and Trademark Office by International Bible Society.

Scripture quotations marked TLB are taken from *The Living Bible,* copyright © 1971 owned by assignment by KNT Charitable Trust. All rights reserved.

Chapter 20, "Boring Barry: The Kid without a Story" by Greg Johnson, first appeared in *Breakaway* magazine, July 1990.

Chapter 31, "Being Different Makes a Difference!" by Susie Shellenberger, first appeared in *Sharing My Faith,* published by Beacon Hill Press, Kansas City. Copyright © 1991.

Lyrics to "Be the One" on pages 197-198 by Al Denson, Dave Clark, and Don Koch, copyright © 1990 Paragon Music Corp./ASCAP, John T. Benson Pub. Co./ASCAP, First Verse Music/ASCAP. All rights reserved. Used by permission of Benson Music Group, Inc.

"Your Most Important Relationship," pages 201-204, is taken from a booklet by the same name published by Campus Crusade. Copyright © 1985 Youth for Christ/USA and Campus Crusade for Christ International. Used by permission.

Stuff at the End of the Book #5, "How Possessive Are You?" first appeared in *Brio* magazine, January 1993.

Library of Congress Cataloging-in-Publication Data

Johnson, Greg, date
   Keeping your cool while sharing your faith / Greg Johnson and Susie Shellenberger.
     p. cm.
   Summary: Provides inspiration and methods for young people to lead Christian lives and share their faith with others.
   ISBN 0-8423-7036-6
   1. Witness bearing (Christianity)—Juvenile literature. [1. Christian life.] I. Shellenberger, Susie. II. Title.
BV4520.J55   1993
248′.5—dc20   93-7532

Printed in the United States of America

99
7   6

For Cheryl Stevens

~~You gave me the key to your house, and I felt included. You gave me your family and I felt trusted. You gave me yourself, and I was loved.~~
~~Thank you.~~

(NAH. TOO SYRUPY. SOUNDS LIKE A GREETING CARD.)

~~I could go on and on about everything you've done for me: teaching me how to make killer soufflé, flying with me to Jackson Hole, Wyoming, at the last minute, cleaning my carpet, feeding Jamaica, bringing all the new single guys to *my* Sunday school class, loaning me the Jacuzzi . . .~~
~~But the bottom line is: You have been Jesus to me. And though the fun times make me laugh . . . your life-style makes me think. You have challenged me. I have grown.~~
Thank you.

(ALMOST, BUT NOT QUITE.)

Remember the first time we walked? You got blisters after the third mile. Now, two years later, you have walked the world with me: to the water tower, around ball parks, neighborhood streets—even through a few dark tunnels. The neat part? When it got reeeeeally scary, you provided the light.

For our *friendship* and *accountability,* I'll forever be grateful.

(YEP. THAT'S IT. GOOD DEDICATION.)

— *Susie*

To Ron Buck, Ed Daniels, and Sean McCartin. Don't forget, LUG tomorrow morning at 6:30. Ron, you bring the bread; Ed, you bring the OJ; and Sean, we need two dozen eggs. Thanks for making Campus Life so great at Elmira. You lived a lot of this book.

Greg

Here's the Stuff

(It looks like a lot, but every

That's in This Book

A Small Part of Your Brain, Please!

Mitch shifted his '87 Escort into "park" and turned off the ignition. Youth group tonight had flooded his mind with a thousand questions. His hands moved to the steering wheel and gripped it tightly. His eyes fixed on the garage light that illuminated the steps leading to the front door of his house. It was late, but he couldn't reach for the door handle and get out . . . not yet.

"What do you care about *so much* that you'd die for it?" his youth leader had asked.

While a few friends whispered in the back—like always—Mitch had stared intently at the brown paneling beyond the leader's shoulder and allowed that question to soak in.

I'd die for me, Mitch thought to himself. *I'd die for Mom and Dad.*

"I know you'd die for your family," the leader interrupted while Mitch was still trying to decide whether his older brother was worth dying for, "but have you ever thought about dying TO something?"

Huh? What does he mean? Die TO something?

"To the thought that the world revolves around you; that you're the most important person to worry about."

The rest of the talk gave a half-dozen examples of how it's normal—but dangerous—to always be thinking about yourself . . . and not really thinking—or caring—for others.

He ended with a statistic that stuck in Mitch's mind: "Do you realize that 95 percent of us think about how to get our own needs met 95 percent of our waking hours? What will it take for you to be one of the 5 percent who'll think about others at least 10 to 20 percent of the time? Or will you always be too busy living for *you* to really help someone else?"

If it had been anyone else saying those things Mitch would have blown it off like a hundred other talks he'd heard. But he knew his youth leader—and he knew he wasn't just trying to make them feel guilty so they'd invite a friend to the fall retreat. This guy cared for others. He wanted his group to care, too.

As Mitch peeled his hands from the wheel and opened the door, he made a decision about what he'd heard.

He decided that tomorrow he'd think about it again.

Who's Got the Time to Think?

To God, you're the most important person in the world. He allowed his Son, Jesus, to die on a cross to prove it. Since God thinks you're important, you should, too. Right?

From the looks of things, that's about how we act. Our whole life seems to revolve around us. Let's take a quick peek at what we care about most as we stumble out of bed and head through the day:

1. (If you're a girl:) Your looks come first. You shower, style your hair, put on makeup, pick out the right clothes, make sure everything is in place, then head off to the kitchen for something light to eat.

   (If you're a guy:) You head down to the cupboards and have your standard two bowls of cereal, a piece of toast, and chocolate milk. Then you hit the shower, put on something comfortable, comb your hair, brush your teeth, and head out the door.

2. At school, you've got classes to be on time for, homework to turn in, lectures to stay awake through, and new assignments you can't miss.

3. Lunch arrives and you've got those hunger pangs to fix. Plus you have to find your friends so you're not walking the halls by yourself.

4. Then it's more classes, and finally time to head home—or maybe participate in an activity like sports or band. Usually, after-school stuff is competitive. You've got to perform your best or someone will take your place.

5. Back at the ranch, there's homework, chores, and dinner.

6. Finally, it's six-thirty. You've been up for twelve hours and you've made it through another day. Everything you've done has revolved around the schedule some-

one else has given you. Now it's time to relax, talk on the phone, watch TV, listen to music—do stuff you LIKE to do, not stuff you HAVE to do.

7. By nine or ten, it's off to dreamland so you'll be ready for another day of the same routine.

What's Missing?

Besides the time you spend with friends or relaxing, realistically there isn't much time for anyone ▼

else. So why even worry about not having time to help others—there's barely a minute to consider it anyway, right?

On the surface, that's pretty true. Especially these days when *every* teen seems ultra-busy. If you throw a job into the above mix of priorities then it *really* seems like there isn't ANY TIME for anyone else.

Or is there?

While your schedule may be so jam-packed that not even your mom could find a spare minute to help

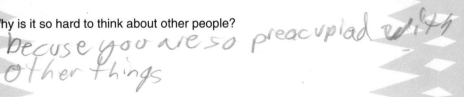

Reflecting . . .

1 What are the most important things in *your* life?

God, Family, Friends

2 Is there anything you need to *decrease* in importance?

Friends

3 Is there anything you need to *increase* in importance?

God Family

4 Why is it so hard to think about other people?

becuse you are so preacupiad with other things

others, you *do* have a space in your brain where you can think.

At the beginning of this book, that's all we're asking you to do: carve out a small, unused portion of your thought time to consider a few things about you and your friends . . . and especially consider how you can be the best friend—to all of your friends—that God wants you to be. That's all. No arm-twisting, threats, condemnation, or guilt. Honest.

The journey we're going to guide you through starts in the brain anyway. If you don't have time to even *think* about others, you certainly don't have time to try to *help* them. So plug your brain into the next few pages as we throw a few of *our* thoughts into *your* thoughts.

xii

Choose Your Own Intro

Most books have a beginning and an end. This one does too. But ours is *different* because we're letting you choose your *own* beginning.

Works like this:

You already know this is a book about learning how to share your faith without being a geek, caring about your friends, caring about yourself, how to make homemade Fudgsicles (just kiddin'! wanted to make sure you were still with me), and deepening your relationship with Christ.

Since everyone reading this book is different, we want you to start with a chapter you're interested in, then jump into the journey with us.

So . . . when talking about sharing your faith (since that's the main reason for this book), what motivates *you* to share? What makes you care enough to want your non-Christian friends to know about your relationship with God?

Choose your own beginning:

"Because I feel guilty if I don't do *anything.*" (Turn to chapter 1, page 1.)

"Because it's the right thing to do." (Turn to chapter 2, page 5.)

"Because I don't want my friends going to hell! And that's exactly where they're headed if they don't know the Lord." (Turn to chapter 3, page 9.)

"Well . . . I *want* to share God with those around me, but I'm too shy." (Turn to chapter 4, page 13.)

"Because God's Word *tells* me to share my faith." (Turn to chapter 5, page 19.)

Reflecting . . .

1 What motivates you the most to try stepping out of the comfort zone and sharing your faith?

Seeing how bad the peace
that no crist are.
^don't

We Won't Tell Anyone

Someone handed you this book and said, "Read it."

Now, after glancing through the "Stuff in This Book" section, reading the "Start Here" chapter, and then flipping through to *this* page, you know what you're about to be hit with: sharing your faith.

I know. I know. *Some* of you are saying, *"Ugh!* First my parents, then my youth leader, next the speaker at last summer's camp, now *these* two strangers. Won't anyone just leave me alone?"

You believe sharing Christ with others is a good idea for *some* Christians. It's just not right for *you*. You have too many things to worry about besides helping others believe in Jesus. Yes, and you even know it's kinda selfish NOT to think about helping your friends get closer to

God. But at this moment in time, you just can't help it.

Hey, we understand completely. And we even want to help. Instead of reading this whole book, here's something you can memorize in case anyone corners you and asks what the book was about. You can say:

What I really liked about it was the short, easy-to-read chapters. It started off by talking about all the different reasons to share your faith: the Bible, hell, it's fun to help others, stuff like that.

Then they talked about the things that get in the way of doing it: being shy, fearing rejection, not knowing what to say or how to say it.

Finally, they talked about

how to do it. They gave a whole bunch of practical suggestions, too: asking the right questions, being there even when a friend is pushing you away, inviting them to different types of Christian things.

It was really good. Here, why don't you give it to someone else so they can read it, too?

That's all it'll take. And you don't have to feel guilty, either, because we gave you permission to say it.

But remember, this is ONLY if they ask "What was the book about?" not "Did you read the book?" If you give this answer to *that* question . . . well, you'll be lying.

But just in case you're not sleepy enough yet to put this book down, push on ahead to the next few chapters. Then if you don't like it, you can honestly say, "I read the first few chapters, and it really didn't capture my attention. Here, give it to someone else."

xvi

The Guilt-Man Cometh

Jamie squirmed. Gary, her youth leader, was saying some pretty strong stuff. "If you knew Tom Cruise, Paula Abdul, or Michael Jordan *personally,* wouldn't you want to *tell* someone?"

Sure, Jamie thought. *I'd brag about it to EVERYONE!*

"I would," Gary continued. "In fact I'd probably tend to go a little overboard, like having T-shirts made that read, 'I'm personal friends with Michael Jordan.'"

Yeah, Jamie reasoned. *I'd probably wear a button or something so everyone around me would know that I'm tight with Tom.* Then she giggled to herself. *Imagine!*

"Think about it," Gary challenged. "I'd want to scream to the world that the man who's tagged as walking on air is my *pal.* But think about this," he continued. "Who's

more important? The man who *seems* to walk on air . . . or the one who *invented* air?

"Michael Jordan may look like he defies gravity, but I'm personal friends with the one who *created* gravity. And what's tougher? To give

1

the *illusion* of soaring through the air to dunk a basketball, or to *actually* walk on water and perform miracles?"

Wow! Never thought about it that way, Jamie thought.

"Obviously, our relationship with the Master of the Universe is tremendously more important than any friendship we could have with another human being. You're on a first-name basis with *GOD!* So don't you want to *tell* someone?"

Jamie squirmed again. *That's true. I mean, Jesus is the most important person I could ever know. How come I don't get as excited about sharing my relationship with him as I would about sharing my friendship with Tom Cruise? (That is, if I actually knew TC.)*

"So what are you going to do? Wear a shirt? Carry a Bible? Make some buttons or posters?" Gary asked. "How 'bout something a little more practical? Why not just be ready to share your faith when someone seems interested?

"Some practical and easy ways would be to invite them to youth group, answer their questions when they ask about the difference in your life, and make sure your lifestyle reflects Jesus himself."

Jamie squirmed again. She loved coming to youth group, but when Gary talked about sharing their faith, it always made her a little nervous. Still . . . everything he was saying made a lot of sense.

"If *you* don't share Jesus with those around you, who will?" Gary challenged. "Again, I'm asking you to think tonight. Think *hard* for a few minutes, OK? *You* may be the only 'Bible' that your classmates see. If they're from a non-Christian family and don't attend church, *you're* the only contact they have with the Answer to their problems.

"Knowing you have the Answer . . . realizing you're plugged into the power source for life's troubles, how can you *not* share him? Why would you *want* to keep his love a secret?

"Here it is—straight and simple—your friends who don't know Christ are headed for hell. Who can stop them? *You can!* Please care enough about your non-Christian friends to brag a little about the most important Person in the world. *You know him personally!* Dare to share your faith. Again . . . if you don't, who will?"

Jamie felt a little guilty. Just yesterday Angie asked her why she always seemed to have her act together. Jamie almost said something about God, but froze because she wasn't quite sure *what* to say.

Then today on the bus, Richie complained about being bored over the weekend. *That would've been* the perfect time for me to invite him to our youth group retreat next weekend, Jamie realized.

Lord, she prayed silently, *I'm proud that I know you. Help me not to keep your Good News a secret any longer. When you bring obvious opportunities my way, help me to take advantage of them and share you with those around me.*

I feel guilty, she continued, *for not taking advantage of the situations you've placed me in. I realize if my friends don't know you, they're going to spend forever in hell. Give me the courage to care enough to speak out. Amen.*

Jamie left youth group that night with a new sense of purpose. She was now on a mission. *Wow!* she thought as she said good-bye to her church friends. *I actually KNOW the Ruler of the World! That kinda makes everything else pale in comparison. To think that the Lord of lords—the one everyone will someday bow before—is my Best Friend. . . . How can I keep that a secret?*

I won't! she determined.

Reflecting . . .

1 Name a few celebs you'd be pretty excited about knowing.

Tom hanks Tom crosie mel Gibsion

2 What person in your life are you the most proud to know?

my mom

3 Who is the most proud to know you?

my parents

4 Was the youth leader fair in what he was saying?

tottaly

Jumping In without a Life Jacket

Four days of camp, only one left to go, and nearly everyone was ignoring me. That's just the way I liked it.

Then on Thursday after lunch I was lying on my bunk, getting ready to head off into dreamland, when six guys burst into the cabin. One said, "Where is he?"

Turning my face toward the wall, I tried to ignore them . . . hoping they'd ignore me. But like a fool, I chanced a quick glance over my left shoulder.

"There he is!"

I moaned a big *ugh*. I'd been discovered.

"Hey, Perry, we want you to go down the river with us this afternoon. There's a ton of white water, and we think it's about time you start joining in."

"Sorry, guys," I said. "I can't swim."

"No problemo, you'll be wearing a life jacket. Besides, no one has fallen out of a boat all week. We'll take care of you. You have to go. No more discussion. See you at three o'clock—sharp!"

I spent the rest of the afternoon

5

convincing myself I couldn't go through with it. But of course I had to. Even a shy guy like me has a male ego to protect. The last thing I needed was to be labeled a chicken.

As I wandered down to the river, I was certain I could talk them out of it. But when I got there it looked like that wasn't going to be necessary.

At three o'clock, nine of us showed up at the bank of the Boulder River. I counted the life jackets—there were only eight. Now was my chance to make a graceful escape.

Unfortunately, my luck was striking out. One of the staff members, Rick, said he'd go without a life jacket as long as the guide guaranteed it was safe.

The leader said it might be kind of dangerous to put nine guys in an eight-man raft. . . .

Great!!! I thought.

. . . but since we were all together, he would chance it.

Not so great.

As soon as we put out from the bank, the sinking feeling in my stomach hit bottom. My bad-luck average remained unchanged.

Nine guys in an eight-man raft turned out to be too much weight. Almost immediately it became impossible for us to maneuver the raft where we wanted to go.

The rapid current funneled us toward the bank on the opposite side of the river. Dead trees—jutting out like jousting spears—were everywhere. We avoided the first two, but went full force into the third.

What happened next will be imprinted on my brain for as long as I live.

The front of the boat hit the snag and was pushed three feet underwater. The two guys straddling the front were dumped in the water. Seconds later, the force of the current pushed the boat under the snag. I heard a snap and a few yells, and then all but two of us were past the snag, either in the water or still in the boat, trying to gain control.

No need to guess who the two were who didn't make it past the snag—Rick and me! All of our strength was being spent trying to hang on as tightly as we could to the piece of wood that was now a part of the nightmare.

The terror I felt earlier in the day paled in comparison to the danger we were in now.

Rick stared straight into my eyes and yelled, "I don't know how to swim!"

Great, I thought. *Now I know we're going to die.*

I looked into Rick's eyes and saw that he was surprised at my fear. I had the life jacket and this guy didn't! He should be the one terrified, not me.

The icy water rushing by felt like it was going *through* instead of *around* us. Rick screamed that in order for us to make it to the bank we were going to have to let go. This would allow the current to take us past the wall of tree snags that prevented us from reaching shore.

I couldn't talk. I just clung.

He screamed at me a couple more times with the same message.

I didn't move.

Finally, after what seemed like hours (probably about three minutes), Rick let go. The force of the current carried him down the narrow river, around a bend, and out of sight.

I tightened my grip on the snag, hoping I'd wake up and the nightmare would suddenly end.

A minute or so later, I heard a noise and looked up. There was Rick!!

From the bank he was yelling at me to let go. Though I pretended I didn't hear him, reality began hitting me in the face. I had to make a decision.

I let go! But instead of letting the water take me down the river, I sank! Can you believe it?—I sank!

What happened next I don't really remember. All I know is that when it was over, I was amazed at what had happened.

Rick had been safe on the bank. His fear and the pounding of the ice-cold Montana mountain river were gone. He had escaped.

I'm not really certain he actually thought about what his choices were. For a guy like him, he probably only thought of one. Instead of staying safe on the bank while I drowned, he jumped in after me.

He couldn't swim, and he had no life jacket—yet he jumped in!

A moment later we were moving. And then it was over. Like everyone else in that eight-man raft, we had made it to shore. The nightmare had finally ended.

Though this is a true story, it's not exactly "Rescue 911" material. You've probably heard stories like this one before. There's an emergency situation where someone needs help, and there's only a short amount of time to make a life-or-death decision.

While you may think you've never faced this type of decision before, think again. You're actually faced with this choice every day.

For nine months of the year you pass perhaps hundreds of people your own age in the hallways at school. Most are only nameless faces. Many others are mere acquaintances or people you used to be friends with. A few, however, are your close friends. Though some of these kids go to church, we know church attendance doesn't always mean someone knows the Savior in a personal way.

I don't want to be overdramatic, but I'm sure you realize who is on the bank at your school. It's you . . .

7

and others who are Christians. Perhaps you were pulled out of the water by a friend. Or maybe you've been on the shore for as long as you can remember. Just by looking at most of them, you wouldn't know the other kids at school are drowning. Indeed, some are only drowning in shallow water. They're not that bad—true—but they're still drowning. They need someone like you who is secure on the bank to dive in and bring them safely to shore.

If someone doesn't, they won't drown in a faraway river—they'll spend eternity separated from God. That's what hell is—eternal separation from God.

Then death and Hades were thrown into the lake of fire. The lake of fire is the second death. If anyone's name was not found written in the book of life, he was thrown into the lake of fire. (Revelation 20:14-15)

As the weeds are pulled up and burned in the fire, so it will be at the end of the age. The Son of Man will send out his angels, and they will weed out of his kingdom everything that causes sin and all who do evil. They will throw them into the fiery furnace, where there will be weeping and gnashing of teeth. (Matthew 13:40-42)

While it's God—not us—who ultimately does the saving, he uses Christians who are willing to dive in and discover the joy of bringing someone up from the depths.

Reflecting . . .

1 How is sharing your faith like rescuing people?

beave they are drowding in these of life

2 List three friends who are drowning without Jesus.

Zac, Matt, Clay

3 Can you decide *right now* to pray consistently for them? Who can remind you to do it?

yes, Myself write above

"Hell? You've Gotta Be Kidding!"

OK. OK. I hear ya. **My friends who don't know Christ are going to hell. I've heard that for years. But is hell really that bad?**

Good question. What do *you* think?

Well . . . I'll just tell ya what I've heard, OK?

OK.

I've heard some people say that hell will be whatever makes you the most miserable.

Hmmm. So, if doing homework really ticks you off, hell will be eternal homework?

Yeah, I guess.

That's punishment all right, but do you really think someone like, oh, I don't know, let's say Hitler— who was responsible for *millions* of deaths and human torture—will be sitting around for eternity writing book reports?

When you put it that way, it sounds kinda lame.

Yeah, and hell is not lame. It's beyond our imagination. It's a place we wanna make sure we stay away from.

Well, I've also heard that

someday Jesus will take all the Christians to heaven, and everyone else will be left here on earth and that will be hell because there will be no love or kindness.

Yeah, that'd be pretty bad. But hell is more than simply a void of love and kindness.

So . . . just how bad IS it? And WHAT is it?

The only way we can answer those questions is to take a peek at what Jesus said about hell. He gives a pretty graphic description. In fact, *every* time he mentions hell, he describes it as a place of great torment and agony. He tells us it's an actual *place* . . . a lake of fire.

Yuck.

Yeah. Double yuck. Grab your Bible, OK? Tell me what you think of *this* picture of hell:

"There was a certain rich man," Jesus said, *"who was splendidly clothed and lived each day in mirth and luxury. One day Lazarus, a diseased beggar, was laid at his door. As he lay there longing for scraps from the rich man's table, the dogs would come and lick his open sores. Finally the beggar died and was carried by the angels to be with Abraham in the place of the righteous dead. [Heaven] The rich man also died and was buried, and his soul went into hell. There, in torment, he saw Lazarus in the* far distance with Abraham.

"'Father Abraham,' he shouted, 'have some pity! Send Lazarus over here if only to dip the tip of his finger in water and cool my tongue, for I am in anguish in these flames.'

"But Abraham said to him, 'Son, remember that during your lifetime you had everything you wanted, and Lazarus had nothing. So now he is here being comforted and you are in anguish. And besides, there is a great chasm [distance] separating us, and anyone wanting to come to you from here is stopped at its edge; and no one over there can cross to us.'

"Then the rich man said, 'O Father Abraham, then please send him to my father's home—for I have five brothers—to warn them about this place of torment lest they come here when they die.'

"But Abraham said, 'The Scriptures have warned them again and again. Your brothers can read them any time they want to.'

"The rich man replied, 'No, Father Abraham, they won't bother to read them. But if someone is sent to them from the dead, then they will turn from their sins.'

"But Abraham said, 'If they won't listen to Moses and the prophets, they won't listen even though someone rises from the dead.'" (Luke 16:19-31, TLB)

Pretty plain, huh?

Yeah. I don't like that.

I'm glad. You *shouldn't* like it. Hell is not going to be a big party.

But I hear my non-Christian friends joke and say they're all going to hell together. They laugh about all the stuff they're gonna do with no one to stop them.

The truth is, people won't even recognize each other in hell. I can't imagine how tremendously painful it would be to burn forever in flames of fire that can't be extinguished—and never have relief—but it's *not* going to be party time!

Wow. That sounds so strong.

Yeah . . . it does. But every single time Jesus talks about hell, he uses strong language to describe it.

Guess that's because he wants to make sure we stay away from it, huh?

Yep.

You know . . . I hear the word *hell* a lot. I mean, kids at school toss it around so casually. Is that right?

Nope. They're using it as a cuss word. They've reduced an actual place to a mere slang term. And you're right . . . it's a word we hear often—on TV, in the hallways, at work—but again, remember the *truth*. Hell is not simply an expression to use when you're angry. It's an actual *place* where people who don't know Christ will spend eternity.

Whew! That's strong.

Yeah. Hell is heavy. It's not a laughing matter. Know what else is heavy?

What?

Millions around us are dying spiritually. They're searching for answers, for truth, and for peace. We have the answers. We know the Truth when we know Christ. They're headed for hell, and it's up to us to point them in the right direction.

I usually don't think about it that seriously. I mean, I know the kids at my school who aren't Christians, but it's usually pretty easy to just shrug it off. After all, if they wanna party and mess around, I can't stop 'em.

Yeah, but see, the reason they're partying and messing around is because they're seriously searching for some answers . . . for peace, for joy.

Think they even realize they're searching for something?

Probably not. But it's obvious, isn't it?

Yep.

And the heavy part is, *we* have the answers. *We* can make a positive difference in their lives. *We* can help point them in the right direction!

Yeah, I WANT to . . . I'm just scared. (But don't tell anyone I said that!)

Hey, this is just between you and me, OK?

OK. Good.

It's OK to be scared.

It is?

Sure! That's normal.

Whew! Feels good to be normal.

Probably *everyone's* a little nervous when it comes to talking about our faith . . . because our relationship with Christ is a personal thing. It's important to us. Sometimes it's kind of hard to put into words.

Yeah! That's exactly how I feel. And besides, I never know what to say.

You're on the right track.

Whaddya mean?

You've got this book, right?

So?

So that's what the next few pages are all about . . . how to share your faith. Keep reading. I think you're gonna like this.

I think I am, too.

But before you go any farther, take a break. You deserve a Coke for reading this far.

Reflecting . . .

1 What do most of your friends think hell is—a party place, cuss word, lake of fire, nonexistent?

cuss word

2 What do you imagine hell to be like?

The etarnal pain

3 Has reading this chapter changed your concept of hell?

kind of

"But I'm Too Shy!"

Brian wasn't Mr. Popular. In fact, he only had three close friends—and they all went to church. Sure, he knew lots of other kids, but he wasn't sure he wanted more friends. He was happy with the few he had. Besides, he didn't know what to say to someone one-on-one. He'd be too nervous. And it was really hard trying to break into other groups. He didn't need the rejection in case they decided he didn't fit in. It just wasn't worth it.

Brian has it tough, doesn't he? He's not hurting anyone. He's being a good friend to the guys he spends time with. He goes to church and youth group. What more does God want out of him?

Probably nothing. If God made him shy, he doesn't expect him to try expanding his friendships. Shy

Christians are different. They can—with God's blessing—just stay with the Christian friends they have.

(Turn the page for an important announcement for all of you shy people.)

HOW TO OVERCOME SHYNESS

Since shy people don't have to read any more of this book, they are free to grab a Magic Marker and use these pages to doodle on.

Those of you who are outgoing— or are outgoing wannabes— this is no time to take a break. Keep reading!!!

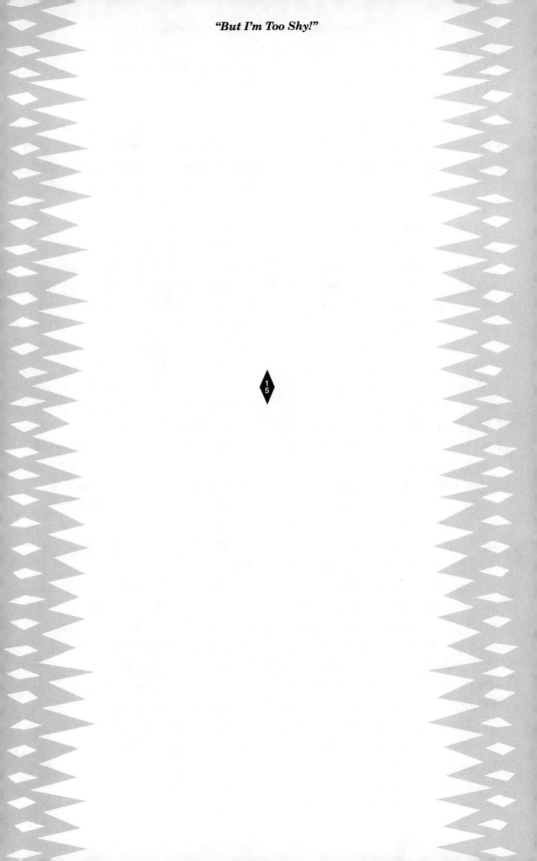

WRONG!

Though some shy Christians may want an out, many don't. Some really desire to let others know they're Christians. Here's a letter *Brio* magazine received from one girl:

Dear Susie:

I'm really shy about announcing my faith. Unless I'm around my Christian friends, I never speak of my personal morals and beliefs. I want to share my joy with my non-Christian friends, but how do I do so without pushing Christianity onto them?

—REDDING, CALIFORNIA

For those shy folk who breathed a sigh of relief a couple of pages ago at being let off easy, it's time to inhale. No, you don't have to hold your breath in fear because we're not going to tell you to break out of your shell and be more outgoing. The reason: Each of us has a personality that's shaped from when we're a child. Often, we take on the characteristics of our parents. Yes, it's true that some can overcome their shyness and learn to be more outgoing, but many don't. That's OK.

Whether *you* want to be less shy or not, being a genuine friend has nothing to do with how well you speak in public, how much you talk in new situations, or how many parties you're invited to.

God has made you and your personality unique for a reason. Some people only warm up to others who are also shy. Shy people are afraid of rejection, so they tend to become loners. They sit alone in the cafeteria, do their homework, and go home. They might be intimidated by overbearing, super-outgoing people, but another shy person may be able to reach them.

We're not going to ask you to gather all of these shy people together and start a "Bashful Brigade." Instead, learn these two skills that will make you one of the best friends a shy person ever had: *watch people* and *ask questions*.

At the beginning of the school year or a new semester, look for the new people in your grade. Start observing the guy or girl who always walks the hallways alone. Then do something that may not naturally fit your personality—go up to him or her and ask a few basic questions.

"Hi, my name's Mary, what's yours?"

"What school did you go to last year?"

"How do you like your schedule? What teachers do you have?"

"Well, gotta get to class, I'll see you around . . . Paula, right? I'll try not to forget. Later."

This approach is a harmless and quick way to see if the other person can carry on a conversation—and if they're interested in making new friends. You haven't promised you'll take them to the football game, but you've opened the door the next time you see them in the hallway or the lunchroom.

When you *do* see them next, don't worry if you can't remember their name. Try something like this:

"OK, pop quiz. Can you remember my name? You win, but I forgot yours!" (Or, "I can't remember yours either.")

Now may be the time to either ask a few more harmless questions about classes or where they live . . . or say you'll meet them in the cafeteria for lunch sometime, if they want.

What you're doing is breaking up the ground for a possible friendship. Now remember, your goal doesn't have to be to lead them to Christ the first week (or month or year). Never look at a person as a project. That puts too much pressure on you—and they'll likely see through it fairly soon. Instead, look at them as a potential friend who one day may want to consider your Best Friend in heaven. If they don't, that doesn't mean you should quit being friends with them—they're just not ready yet.

Hopefully, they won't dump you because of your faith (when they find out you have one), but there *is* that possibility. If that happens, you haven't failed—it only means there's someone else who needs you more. Keep trying.

Take Others with You

Like Brian in the first paragraph of this chapter, you probably already have a small group of friends you hang out with. If one of them is also a Christian, try meeting new friends together. It's not only a little safer, but you don't have to try to think of all the questions yourself!

In Luke 10:1-20, Jesus sent out seventy of his followers to the surrounding cities to tell people the

17

— Reflecting . . . —

1 What frightens you the most about sharing your faith?

Someone will make fun of it

2 How can shy people ask someone else questions and not feel weird?

Do it slower like just saying hi

kingdom of heaven was at hand. He sent them two by two. He must have known that it's better for two to walk together. The response they saw was incredible!

Whether you try to meet new friends with a buddy or by yourself, one thing is certain: God isn't expecting you to skate through every school day being content with the same group of friends. He's got bigger plans for your shy personality.

The Bible Tells Me So

If you're the type who believes the Ten Commandments were actually "Ten Suggestions," then you're probably not going to be too impressed with this short chapter. Yes, there are certain passages that give a little room for discussion on whether they're actually commands or suggestions, but many don't (like the Ten Commandments).

Of course, if you've never read these next few passages, you couldn't be faulted for not following instructions. But if you *are* a little curious about what the Bible says is a major priority of a Christian, read on.

Let's start with what's known as "the great commission."

Therefore go and make disciples of all nations, baptizing them in the name of the Father and of the Son and of the Holy Spirit, and teaching them to obey everything I

have commanded you. And surely I am with you always, to the very end of the age. (Matthew 28:19-20)

They were some of the last words Jesus spoke to his disciples. Today, some Christians actually believe those words only applied to the disciples. If

that's true, then the last part ("I will be with you always") applies only to the disciples, too.

How about these words from Jesus early in his ministry:

The harvest is plentiful but the workers are few. Ask the Lord of the harvest, therefore, to send out workers into his harvest field. (Matthew 9:37-38)

Whether you realize it or not, someone has prayed for you to enter the harvest. Will you choose to be the answer to their prayer?

Here's a couple more words from Jesus. Not as direct, but just as true:

You are the light of the world. A city on a hill cannot be hidden. Neither do people light a lamp and put it under a bowl. Instead they put it on its stand, and it gives light to everyone in the house. In the same way, let your light shine before men, that they may see your good deeds and praise your Father in heaven. (Matthew 5:14-16)

You did not choose me, but I chose you and appointed you to go and bear fruit—fruit that will last. (John 15:16)

Being a "light-fruit" doesn't mean we're a dwarf peach. It means that God has graciously allowed us to become Christians. Why? So we'll attract people to him in a way that will make them want to stick with the faith for a lifetime, not just a few months.

How about these "suggestions" from the apostle Paul:

Preach the Word; be prepared in season and out of season; correct, rebuke and encourage—with great patience and careful instruction. (2 Timothy 4:2)

Therefore, if anyone is in Christ, he is a new creation; the old has gone, the new has come! All this is from God, who reconciled us to himself through Christ and gave us the ministry of reconciliation: that God was reconciling the world to himself in Christ, not counting men's sins against them. And he has committed to us the message of reconciliation. We are therefore Christ's ambassadors, as though God were making his appeal through us. (2 Corinthians 5:17-20)

Here's a short explanation of this passage: If we're Christians, we *have been* given a message and a ministry—reconciliation. It means to bring one person back into peace with another (your friend and God). We're also ambassadors—we represent God here on earth just as the U.S. ambassador to Canada represents the president of the United States. It's like, "He couldn't be here, so he sent me." God can't physically be in your school, so he sent you.

Paul also gives this pretty much fool-proof argument:

How, then, can they call on the one they have not believed in? And how can they believe in the one of whom they have not heard? And how can they hear without someone preaching to them? And how can they preach unless they are sent? As it is written, "How beautiful are the feet of those who bring good news!" (Romans 10:14-15)

So, how beautiful are *your* feet?

Here's a final word from the apostle Peter:

But in your hearts set apart Christ as Lord. Always be prepared to give an answer to everyone who asks you to give the reason for the hope that you have. But do this with gentleness and respect. (1 Peter 3:15)

Got the Picture?

There are other passages that aren't so direct, but we think you get the idea. The Bible has A LOT to say about our role as a participant with God in making sure others at least hear about Jesus and what he's done for us.

Now, like other direct commands in Scripture, we can choose to ignore or disobey them. God doesn't arm-wrestle us into obedience; instead, he waits until our heart and mind finally get around to agreeing with what he's already said. For some Christians, in this area especially, their heart and mind never get around to it. To us, that's sad. We've found there is no greater joy than being available to be used by God in moving those around us one more notch up the faith ladder. In fact, if all God wanted from us was to accept him and go to church, he could have transported us to heaven the moment we became Christians.

But he left us here, didn't he? The passages you've just read tell you why.

Reflecting . . .

1. Why do so few Christians actually obey these passages?

they think that am a christ dant now Its over with

"I Don't Give a Twit!"

Your friends are going to hell. The Bible says to play "show-and-tell" with your faith. It's fun to help others. Your youth leader says it's a good idea . . . so that settles it: the time is NOW. You're going to start doing all you can to help your friends understand everything about God, Jesus, and the Bible. Enough said. Right?

Well, probably not for everyone glancing through these pages.

Even though you may intellectually believe all those great arguments—you may be one who still could care twit about helping others or sharing your faith with friends. That doesn't mean you're not a Christian, it just means you haven't developed the heart and desire— yet. And if your parents or other Christian friends don't have that type of heart around you, how are you going to get it?

Good question.

Let's see, you could:

a. Buy it from Susie (cashier's checks only).

b. Go to the beach and hope you find it washed up on the shore.

c. Listen to every Al Denson,

23

Steve Camp, and Keith Green tape you can get your hands on.

d. Stay in bed 'til God gives it to you (hey, let's think about that one a little longer).

e. Hope Ed McMahon sends it to you . . . along with ten million dollars.

f. Try to play your mom's Elvis records backwards and listen for "The Message."

OR, you could put up with Greg for a second while he tries to get mildly analytical.

For the next two minutes, pretend you *really* like tennis—A LOT! In order to get to the advanced state of tennis fanatic, there were some stages you unknowingly went through.

1. **You heard about it.** Somewhere in your past you learned that tennis was a sport that might be fun.

2. **You watched it from a distance.** Maybe you saw it on TV or drove by the local junior high and watched kids your age chasing down a soft green ball with a racket. It looked hard . . . but also kinda fun.

3. **You watched it up close.** Instead of observing from a distance, you went to the courts a couple of times and took in the action firsthand.

4. **You tried it with help and encouragement.** "Dad, do you think you can teach me how to play tennis?" you asked a few days later.

"Sure. We'll borrow your brother's racket and go hit a few balls next Saturday," he responded enthusiastically.

So you went out with your dad, and he taught you how to hold the racket, showed you some footwork, demonstrated some follow-through, and pretty soon you were hitting the ball ten times in a row *off* the practice wall instead of *over* it. You knew you were ready for the courts.

Then came the risky part.

5. **You tried playing your older brother—alone.** But your dad came to watch and even coach a little. Your brother easily smashed you six to nothing— but you still thought tennis was fun enough to keep practicing.

6. **Tennis soon became something you were pretty good at. You decided to keep playing.** Even though you'll never be a Jennifer Capriati or Andre Agassi, you made the school team your junior year.

This process of building a love for something is the same whether it's mastering a sport, playing a musical instrument, tying flies, acing chemistry, blowing bubbles, shaving (your legs or your face) . . . even relating to the opposite sex. It's also true in learning to care for people—the type of care that's willing *and* eager to share the most important Person in your life with the most important people in your life. Let's see how the illustration relates to sharing your faith.

1. **You hear about sharing your faith (from this book, your youth leader, the Bible, whatever).** Though you're not 100 percent certain what it is, how to do it, or even whether it's worth the risk, at least *now* you know it's something to check into.

2. **You watch others do it from a distance.** Perhaps you've seen a parent, a friend, or your youth leader's wife do out-of-the-ordinary things to help others. You think, *Hey, they're still smiling . . . and they didn't even get spit on.*

3. **You watch others up close.** You go with your dad as he delivers a box of food to some struggling people in your neighborhood. He tells them the food is from Jesus Christ, and a brief conversation ensues between him and the family's father. It's nothing heavy, just a brief explanation of what he meant and a promise to be back with more in a couple of weeks.

4. **You try it yourself—with some encouragement.** You're in the locker room and someone you barely know two lockers down just realizes he left his gym shoes at home. "If I don't dress down for P.E. one more time," you hear him say, "I'm going to flunk!" You don't know him very well, but you see how frustratred he is. And since you have an extra pair of gym shoes in your locker, you make the offer. He accepts.

5. **You practice being a friend—and no one's around to coach you on how to do it.** The next week you see that same person close to your locker and you make small talk about teachers, P.E., and the football game this Friday. He asks if you're going, and you respond, "Yep. Need a ride?" He says he does.

   You've just started a friendship with someone who used to be a stranger. Maybe one day, if the time is right, you'll be able to share your faith with him.

6. **Pretty soon you're trying to renew old junior high acquaintances, as well as make new ones.** You've caught on to this friendship

thing, and you realize that once high school is out, you'll probably never see these folks again. You come to the conclusion that God really can use you to move others one step closer to faith in him—just by going out of your way once in a while and being friendly to others.

It Doesn't Happen Overnight

Building a love for anything—including sharing your faith—will take some time. It starts with that first step, then the second, the third, and so on. If you've been stuck on

the first step for a while, you need to try something that's unique to sharing your faith: Pray about it.

Begin to let God know you'd like to put your toes in the water to see how it feels. Once he knows you're serious, he'll oblige pretty quickly. Honest. No, he's not going to have you street-witnessing or handing out tracts at the bus stop by next Monday (that's a little too fast for most people), but he *will* begin to put people and situations in your life so you can start practicing. That's not too risky, is it?

Reflecting . . .

1 List three positive things that can happen as a result of daring to share your faith with a friend.

You could bring one person ... he could ... purpose ... and ... People would be ... we did

2 What step are you on in building a love for sharing your faith?

6

3 How can you move up another notch?

Let's Talk about God and You

Ever heard the phrase, "God loves you"?

'Course I have. Everyone has. It's not just a phrase; it's probably the most famous Bible verse in the world: John 3:16.

Yeah, and you probably even have it memorized, but do you really *believe* it?

Sure. God loves me. I mean . . . he kinda has to, doesn't he?

What're you talking about?

Well, he's God. It's his job to be nice. I mean, he doesn't really love me because of *me* or anything . . . he just loves me because he loves everyone and that's God's job.

Not!

OK. 'Splain it.

God doesn't *owe* you anything! He's GOD. Creator of the Universe!

King of kings. He loves you because he *wants* to.

I know. I know.

When do you know?

OK, here's an example. Last Sunday I brought someone to church. I know God loved me

for that. And yesterday I smiled at this new kid at school that I don't even know. I could feel God loving me. And just today I did a halfway decent job on my English test. So, yeah . . . I know God loves me.

Whoa! Wait a sec. God doesn't love you because of what you *do!* I mean, if you *never* invited anyone to church he'd love you just as much as if you brought someone new every single week.

And yeah, he's grinning from ear to ear when you flash a smile at someone you don't know. He loves it when you reach out. But he'd love you just the same if you never smiled at all.

And I'm sure he's pleased with your halfway decent English grade. But guess what? He'd love you just as much if you'd bombed.

Go on.

God LOVES you . . . not for what you *do,* but because of who you *are* . . . his precious, valued child.

I'm listening.

He loves you as if you were the only one in all the world to love. Know what that means?

You're doing good, so just keep going, OK?

OK. It means if you were the only person in the entire world, he still would have left the splendor of heaven to walk your dusty streets and die an agonizing death on the cross . . . *just for you!*

Whoa!

And the super-exciting thing is the fact that God *really* loves you! I mean . . . yeah, he loves you when you're doing everything right: winning that class election, completing your homework—even doing boring chores around the house without having to be told. But he *also* loves you when you sass your folks, when you're acting like a jerk—even those times you think about stuff you know you shouldn't be honing in on.

The fact is . . . *he just loves you!*

I love it!

Yeah . . . but now the BIG question.

I got a question comin'?

Do *you* love you?

Yeah. Yeah. Yeah. Sure I love me.

When?

Well . . . Tuesday I did the best time on the mile that I've ever done. Felt great. And last week I put some of my spending money in the offering at church. And just yesterday I remembered my mom's birthday. I'm doin' pretty good.

What about last Thursday?

What about it?

You cheated on your math test.

Hey! How'd you know about that?

And Monday you spread some gossip about Kim.

Yeah, but Kim's a twirp!

And just today you screamed at your sister and told her she was a lousy pest.

She's always coming into my room!

Did you love yourself during those times?

No.

Why not?

It doesn't take a genius to figure this out. You're an adult, you know this.

Yeah, but I'm the one writing the book . . . so go along with me. You want different answers, *you* write a book.

OK. OK.

So?

OK, so I don't love myself when I blow it.

Glad you were honest.

Well, does anyone love themselves when they blow it?

It's a process.

Meaning . . . ?

It might take a while, but that's exactly what God wants to help you with.

God wants me to love myself when I'm a jerk?

Yep.

Why?

'Cause *HE* loves you when you're a jerk. And if GOD not only loves you when you do gr-r-reat, but when you blow it . . . doesn't that mean YOU should love you during those times, too?

I'm thinking.

If the *Creator of the Universe* loves you during your dark moments *as well as* your bright moments, then who are *you* to choose when you'll love yourself? Aren't you supposed to reflect God? To do as he does? To love as he loves?

I'm still thinking.

You have a decision to make.

I hate decisions. Let's go get a Coke instead.

Stick with me. The book can't continue unless you get this part, OK?

OK. OK.

Your decision: When you blow it (and *everyone* does), you can either be your own best friend or your very worst enemy. When you bomb a test what're you going to do? Beat yourself over the back and go on and on about how stupid you are? Or tell yourself, "I'll do better next time. I didn't study enough. I'll ask Jamie to help me. She's terrific at math!"

By saying *positive* things you become your own best friend. You learn to love yourself. By telling yourself *negative* things you become your worst enemy. You begin to hate yourself.

Is that always so bad?

Yep. 'Cause you can't really love *others* until you learn to love and accept yourself.

You're right.

About what?

About this maybe taking some time.

Guess what?

What?

You've got a gr-r-reat Teacher!

You gonna hang around and help me through this?

Only for a few pages. But Jesus . . . well, he's in it for *eternity*.

I love it!

Learn to make Jesus your best friend, and you learn to be friends with yourself as well.

Makes sense.

Learn to fall in love with God more and more each day, and he'll help you love and accept yourself more. And not only when you're winning . . . but when you're losing, too.

Makes even more sense.

And again . . . learn to love *yourself* and you learn to love *others*.

I get it. And the more time I spend with God—like through prayer and reading his Word— *the more I learn to do all that*.

That's exactly right! You don't need this book.

Well . . . I still wanna learn how to share my faith. I mean I've got friends I really care about who don't know God. I want 'em to spend eternity with me in heaven.

Great! Keep reading. This book's just for you.

Will the rest of it be this easy to read?

Yeah. Yeah. Yeah.

Good. 'Cause I'm not into boring stuff or big words.

Neither are I. I mean neither are Greg and I. I mean neither are Greg and me. (Hey, we're not really writers . . . we're just a couple of grown-up kids who love teens.)

What else do you love?

Jumping on trampolines, playing catch with those Velcro paddles and balls, the smell of new tires, eating raw cookie dough . . . but hey, that's another book.

OK. OK. Let's get going.

One more thing.

What's that?

You need to make things right about that test you cheated on.

No way!

Yes way! And guess what?

Gag. What?

Your Best Friend will not only go *with* you . . . he'll even give you the words to say and the strength you'll need.

OK. OK.

So you go straighten out the crooked stuff . . . and I'll meet ya on the next page with a quick quiz that will tell you how good a friend you really are.

OK. But I'm stopping by 7-Eleven to grab an Icee first.

Good. That'll give me a chance to

down some raw cookie dough. Oh, and don't forget to buy a pencil for the quiz!

Wow! This book's gonna be fun!

Reflecting . . .

1 List three things you like about yourself.

am usualy nice
my smile
my attitude toward life

2 What makes it difficult for you to love you?

School

3 Why is it so hard to really believe we don't have to "perform" to get God to love us?

becuse you are taght ever sense you were young theat to get something you have to work hard

4 Do you sometimes have to "perform" at home to feel like your parents accept you?

yes

5 What can you do to realize more that God loves you?

read sertain parts of the Bible

How Good a Friend Are You?

Part of sharing your faith comes with being a good friend—a friend who cares enough to speak out. So let's check your friendship potential, OK? Circle the response that best fits you. Add up your score, and evaluate your friendship style by using the key.

(Note: Some questions say *she* and *her,* and some say *he* and *him.* Don't let that mess you up. Answer *every* question. If you're a guy and you think a particular question was written for a girl, just adapt it in your own mind, OK?)

1. The main quality I look for in a friend is . . .

   a. someone who'll stick by me.

   b. someone I can do stuff with.

   c. someone who's always happy.

   d. someone my size I can trade clothes with.

   e. someone who shares my beliefs.

2. What can tear a friendship apart is when my friend . . .

   a. gossips about me.

   b. won't wear deodorant after gym class.

   c. won't return my phone calls.

   d. steals my boy/girlfriend.

33

e. gets upset over misunder-
standings that are usually
nothing.

3. When my friend is in trouble or has started a bad habit, I'll . . .

a. let her sink or swim—it's
her life.

b. call her mom and make sure
she knows.

c. pray for her.

d. confront her the first chance
I get.

e. ask her about it and let her
know I care.

4. True or False: Real friends never fight. F

5. When I catch a friend lying . . .

a. I want to rip out his tongue.

b. I'll let it pass until it happens again.

c. I make sure he understands
I know the truth.

d. I'll tell everyone he's a liar.

6. If a friend dumps me . . .

a. I'm devastated for a week;
then I get over it.

b. I try to get her back as soon
as I can.

c. I want to talk with her to
find out why.

d. I forget about it and find a
new friend.

7. When my friend is moody . . .

a. I call him a geek and tell
him to get right or get left!

b. I leave him alone and hope
he'll be better the next day.

c. I try to find out what's wrong.

d. I tell everyone to stay away
from him.

e. I give him a lot of attention
so he'll snap out of it.

8. True or False: Once you have a close friend, nothing should ever come between your friendship. F

9. The goal of having friends is to . . .

a. have someone to talk to at
school.

b. make sure they aren't lonely.

c. let them know how much
Christ cares for them.

d. learn how to be a friend.

e. have someone to talk about
behind their back.

10. Being a faithful friend means . . .

a. you'll never reject her no
matter what she does to you.

b. you have to confront her
whenever she does things
that are wrong.

c. never gossiping about her.

d. always defending her in
front of others.

e. being the type of person that
others can share with.

34

Scoring

Give yourself points based on the answers you circled. Add up your score, and look at the results.

1. A = 2, B = 1, C = -1, D = -2, E = 1
2. A = 1, B = -3, C = -1, D = -1, E = 1
3. A = -1, B = -1, C = 3, D = 1, E = 3
4. True = -1, False = 1
5. A = -2, B = 2, C = 2, D = -2
6. A = 1, B = -2, C = 3, D = 2
7. A = -10, B = 2, C = 1, D = -2, E = 1
8. True = 1, False = 2
9. A = -1, B = 1, C = 3, D = 3, E = -2
10. A = 3, B = 1, C = 2, D = 3, E = 2

16–22 points—You need to keep doing what you're doing! As a matter of fact, you ought to reach out more to others. People need friends like you.

11–15 points—You're on the way to becoming the type of friend people want to have. You probably relate well to people but are still a little selfish in your friendships.

Below 11—Somewhere along the line, no one has shown you what a friend really is. Find a caring Christian adult, and ask to learn some skills on how to be a friend.

Bonus Quiz!

If you sometimes have trouble being possessive with your friends, you're not quite through yet. We've got another test designed just for you. You'll find it in the "Stuff at the End of the Book #5" section on page 211. If you're still in a quiz-taking mood, turn to it now. If not, grab your Bible and dig into a few Proverbs and stuff so you can find out what a real friend looks like.

Friendship Guide

Does God's Word have any advice on friendship? You bet! Use the following verses to help you develop better friendships.

- Real friends are few (Proverbs 18:24).
- A friend is someone who really knows you (John 15:15).
- A friend loves you unconditionally (Proverbs 17:17).
- A friend is available for counsel (Proverbs 27:9).
- A friend speaks the truth to you (Proverbs 27:5-6).
- A friend is someone who encourages you (Ecclesiastes 4:9-10).
- A friend is someone who will confront you (Proverbs 27:17).
- A friend is loyal to you (Proverbs 16:28).
- A friend shows real love (1 Corinthians 13:4-7).
- A friend will lay down his life for you (John 15:13).

Tuning In to the Right Station

Dear Susie:

I've been a Christian for a long time, but I still haven't gotten to know God as my personal friend and Father. What can I do? I want to be close to him.

AKRON, OHIO

How do you get close to *any* friend? By spending time with him, talking, and doing things together. What happens as you do these things? You deepen your friendship. You grow closer.

It works the very same way with God. The more you read his letters to you (the Bible), the better you'll understand what he has in store for you. The more time you spend talking with him, the more time you *want* to spend talking with him. And as you bring him into every area of your life (by shooting quick sentence prayers to him all

throughout the day) the more you begin to depend on him.

When your best friend calls you on the phone, I bet you don't have to ask who it is. You can probably tell as soon as she utters the first syllable. She doesn't even have to iden-

37

tify herself. Why? Because you're close. You *know* her.

Guess what? You can know God's voice that clearly, too! He speaks to us in a variety of ways:

- Sometimes through trusted adults who are close to him (like your pastor or youth leader, parents, relatives)
- Through his Word
- And in our mind and in our heart (This is done through his Holy Spirit who lives within us, guiding us in the right direction, helping us to know his will.)

But you know what? It takes *discipline* to learn what his voice sounds like. It means making time d-a-i-l-y to shut everything else out (yep, that means turning off the tube and even the tunes) to focus on his "still, small voice" that comes from *within*.

How do you accomplish this? Through devotions. (Fancy name for reading your Bible and praying. And as you pray—talking with him—don't forget to *listen*.)

When you know the voice of God, BIG things happen! Look at all the people in the Bible who did incredible things simply because they knew God's voice. When God spoke, they acted!

Let's Talk Elijah for a Sec

You remember him, doncha? The guy who challenged President Ahab to a fiery duel over a dead bull? OK, let's do a quick review.

The story's found in 1 Kings 17–19. Mark it in your Bible, OK? But first lemme give you my "Reversed Standard Version." Ever get discouraged because your youth group isn't as big as you wish it was? Elijah could relate. *In a major way!* You see, whenever his youth group had a pizza fling, he was the only teen who showed up.

When they organized money-raising projects (like a car wash or selling tickets to the church chili supper) he was the only one who participated.

Not only that, but when his church had their once-a-month pot-luck dinner . . . you guessed it, he was the only one who brought fried chicken. In fact, he was the only one who showed up!

That's because Elijah was from a reeeeeally small church. We're talkin' itsy-bitsy-teeny-weeny-yellow-polka-dot-bikini-sized church. It was so small, he was the only member.

Yep. *Seemed* like he was the only Christian in the land. (There were really a few more, but he couldn't find them. Kind of like *you* feeling you're the only Christian in your school.)

But Elijah's strength was in *knowing the voice of God*. When God spoke, Elijah acted! Well, God spoke. He told Elijah to tell President Ahab that he was doing a lousy job of running the country, and if he didn't shape up, God would punish the people by withholding the rain. (Bad news, 'cause the crops would wither and die and everyone's stomach would growl and no one would be able to buy Honeycomb or Trix or even Pop-Tarts. So, yeah, it was pretty serious, mon.)

Now, I don't know how *you'd* react if God spoke to *you* and told you to run to the White House and tell *our* president a thing or two . . . but *I* might tend to wonder, *Hmmmm. Was that GOD telling me that? Or was it Satan trying to mess me up and get me to do something really stupid? Or are those just my own thoughts wanting to do something important?*

Elijah didn't have to *wonder* if it was God speaking to him or not. Why? Because *he knew the voice of God!* And he responded IMMEDIATELY.

Yep. Told the president what a twit he was and that God wasn't too pleased with the way things were going and if he didn't make a turn for the better (and get the people to start worshiping God instead of that stupid little statue named Baal) he'd be mighty sorry because a famine would sweep the country and there wouldn't be any rain—which not only meant no crops, but also put a

pretty big damper on summer fun. (Like how can you go water skiing, swimming, tubing, or rafting without *water?* Pretty basic.)

Well, other than talking in run-on sentences, Elijah did a pretty good job of delivering the message. But Prez Ahab didn't listen. (Too busy ordering out for Chinese food.) Next move? God told Elijah to hit the mountains.

Now, the Bible is unclear exactly *which* mountains he fled to, but I live in Colorado Springs—so does Greg—and we both believe that if God were going to send *anyone* to the mountains for a few years, it would probably be the Colorado Rockies. So, let's just assume that's where Elijah went, OK?

I know what you're thinking. *Even the Colorado Rockies can get boring after a few years . . . all alone . . . no food . . . nothing to do.* Wrongo, mountain mamma. The Bible tells us (1 Kings 17:4) that God provided for every one of Elijah's needs. (Kinda neat how he never lets his children go hungry.) We read that the Lord sent ravens to bring him food every day. (Not bad room service, huh? *I* wouldn't mind a few birds flocking by *my* house every morning to drop off Egg McMuffins, a few cans of Dr. Pepper, and a double-thick cheese pizza with Canadian bacon sprinkled on top.)

He had it made! OK . . . he *was* alone. But do you know what I think probably happened? I can imagine God tampering with the power system on the ski lifts—setting the whole thing on automatic—and I can see Elijah popping moguls, doing jumps, and generally having the time of his life.

A few years passed. And just about the time when his parallels were almost perfect (ski term for making reeeeally quick, sharp turns left and right and left and right and . . . well, you get the pix), God spoke. Know what he said? No need to guess; I'll tell ya.

God told Elijah to go back *down* the mountain and talk to Prez Ahab again. (Can't stay on a spiritual mountaintop forever, can we?)

Again . . . I don't know what *you'd* think if God told *you* that. But I think *I* might tend to question, *Nah, that can't be GOD because he's the one who SENT me here! Hmmm. Must be Satan trying to get me away from being where God wants me. Or maybe it's just me wanting to go back home and see my friends and family.*

Elijah had no questions. Didn't doubt for a sec. He *knew* it was God. How? Because *he knew the voice of the Lord.* And when God spoke, he responded!

Well, you can imagine how ol' Ahab reacted when he saw Elijah ▼

heading for the Oval Office! (Actually it's OK if you *can't* imagine it, 'cause I'll fill ya in.)

He pointed his bony finger at God's man and screamed, "You!" (Man of great verbiage, that Ahab.) "You're the one who's responsible for this mess!"

And it really was a mess. Just as Elijah had predicted, God had withheld the rains for several years, people were dying, the crops had withered . . . the country was a disaster.

But Elijah stood his ground. "Back off, Jack!" (Nice attitude.) *"I'm* not the reason for this famine; *you* are! I TOLD you this would happen. God has allowed our country to suffer because of the way you have chosen to rule."

"But . . . but . . . but, I . . ." (Be glad Ahab never spoke for one of your school assemblies. He stammered so much it would've taken *forever* to get his point across!)

"Lissen up, Ahab!" Elijah continued. "Almost the entire country is worshiping Baal. That's not right. God wants to turn the hearts of his people back to *him."*

"But *I'm* not into Baal worship," Ahab defended.

"True. You're not," Elijah agreed. "But you're not into worshiping God, either."

"Well, I, ah . . ."

"Quit stammering, Ahab, and

pay attention!" (Elijah was pretty confident, wasn't he? Would *you* talk to the president that way? Yeah, maybe you would if you knew beyond a shadow of a doubt that God told you to do it. Again—the key? *Knowing the voice of God.*)

"If there's one thing God can't stand, it's a lukewarm commitment," Elijah announced. "Be hot or cold, Ahab, but don't stand in the middle. In other words," (He thought maybe he should make it reeeeally simple in case Ahab was having trouble understanding this part. After all, Ahab wasn't the brightest man around. If he was, he would've been serving God, right?) "Decide to serve Jehovah (fancy old-time name for God) or decide not to, but you can't remain neutral."

"Neutral? But, I, ah . . ." (Yo, Ahab, get a life! Or at least a *language.*)

"Can't ride the fence, Ahab," Elijah warned. "Time to make a decision. What's it gonna be? Serve God? Or worship your silly idols?"

"OK, hold on a second, Elijah. I don't mind serving your God if he's really *God*. But I gotta make sure!" Ahab bargained. "So tell ya what let's do. Let's have a contest. I'll get the four hundred fifty prophets of Baal (pretty big team, huh?), and we'll have a showdown between you and *your* God . . . and them and *their* god."

Sounded like an idea. (Not necessarily a *great* idea—or even a *good* idea because why should we have to *prove* God's existence? Isn't that where *faith* comes in? But it was an IDEA nonetheless.)

So being the creative men they were, they decided on a terrific name. They called it "THE CONTEST." (Wowsers!)

First Church of Baal got majorly excited. They had a humongous youth group. Like over five thousand teens. They decided this would be a great way to earn money for their surf 'n' swim missions trip to Jamaica. (. . . yawn . . .) So they had special T-shirts printed (complete with puff paint) that read "THE CONTEST" and sold 'em for fifteen dollars apiece. They also took charge of the confession stand. I mean, the *concession* stand.

The big day arrived and the Houston Astrodome was literally packed out. (OK, maybe it wasn't the Astrodome, but it was someplace exactly like that. You want a different place, *you* write the next book, OK?)

Mary Carillo—who usually only announced professional tennis matches—was hired to commentate. She went through the rules:

"Since there are more people on the Baal team, we're gonna let them go first. They'll drag their dead bull out here and pray to their god to burn it up. And guys . . . you're aware that you can't use kerosene or charcoal bits, aren't ya? OK, good.

"Then, after they've had a chance to prove the existence of their god, we'll give Elijah a shot with his dead bull. Let the games begin!"

The team of Baal pulled their carcass on stage. (Don't forget the First Church of Baal youth group was selling popcorn, hot dogs, and those giant pretzels. Whoa! They were hauling in the bucks *fer sure.*)

The Baal team members danced around their bull and prayed loudly to their god. People watched closely. Reporters were crouched on the edge of their seats in the press box. Cameras zoomed in extra-close. But nothing happened. The crowd grew restless. (After all, they'd paid big money for this. They wanted to see some action!)

Finally, Elijah grew impatient. And being the good sport he was (tee hee), here's what he said. (And this is straight from *The Living Bible.* I promise. Look it up yourself!)

"You'll have to shout louder than that," he scoffed, *"to catch the attention of your god! Perhaps he is talking to someone, or is out sitting on the toilet, or maybe he is away on a trip, or is asleep and needs to be wakened!"*

(I'm serious. You're gonna have to read it for yourself. I know you don't believe me. Check out 1 Kings 18:27, but be sure you read it from *The Living Bible.*)

And look at what happens *next:*

So they shouted louder and, as was their custom, cut themselves with knives and swords until the blood gushed out. They raved all afternoon until the time of the evening sacrifice, but there was no reply, no voice, no answer. (1 Kings 18:28-29, TLB)

Wow. These guys are serious! They're not just pricking themselves until a little sprinkle of blood drops on their clothes. They're *cutting* themselves with *swords* and *knives* until their blood *gushes out!*

And notice the time! For crying out loud! They've been messing around *all day.* Now it's evening, and still nothing has happened.

So Elijah stepped forward and told the contest helpers to clear the stage. They had to hose it down because of all the blood. As they dragged Elijah's dead bull to center stage, he gave them some weird instructions.

"Dig a trench all the way around the stage and fill it with water," he said. So they did. "Fill it again," he instructed. So they did. "And again," he continued. (*Hmmm.* Filling trenches with water probably isn't the *best* strategy for starting a fire . . . but Elijah was plugged into a mighty power source, remember?)

Finally, they had thrown so much water on stage, the bull was literally lying in a pool of H^{2}O.

Then I can imagine Elijah stepping *away* from the microphone so no one could hear him. I think he probably prayed something like this:

"God, I *know* you're God. I have absolutely no doubt at all that you created this entire universe and you have more power than anything anywhere.

"I'm not asking you to burn this bull to prove your power to me, because—like I said—I'm already convinced of your power. Those doubts were settled a long time ago when I gave my life to you.

"I *am* asking you to burn my bull, though, so these thousands of doubting, questioning, lost people can be convinced that *you* are the only true God."

Then I imagine a hush fell across the stadium. And stepping in front of the mike, Elijah probably boomed in his deepest and loudest voice, "Father God of heaven and earth, BURN THIS BULL!"

Instantly that dead animal was ablaze. It was incredible! People all over the arena began to realize they'd been duped into believing a

false god. They *saw* this power, and they *wanted* what they saw.

It was really neat! Kind of like a Billy Graham Crusade. People just got up from where they were seated and went forward to give their lives to God.

Elijah wasted no time. Microphone still in hand, he exclaimed, "If you came on a bus, it'll wait. If you came with friends, they'll wait. There's nothing more important right now than where you stand with the Creator of the Universe!"

Then he grabbed some of the new converts and convinced them to help him slaughter the prophets of Baal. (I know. I know. It sounds gross. But before Jesus came to die for our sins, God had no choice but to abolish evil through death. So, Elijah knew he *had* to wipe out the Baal gang, or they'd travel to the next town and start the same old thing all over again.)

After all the prophets of Baal were killed, God spoke to Elijah and told him to head back to the mountains. (Back to the mountains? You're kidding! With all *this* action going on? Why? Because God wanted to talk with him, that's why.)

And Elijah didn't question whether it was God's voice, or the voice of Satan, or his own thinking. He responded immediately because (you already know this part, so read it out loud) *he knew the voice of the Lord.*

OK, remember at the first of this chapter when we were talking about God speaking to you? And how it takes d-a-i-l-y discipline to learn the process of *tuning in* to his voice and shutting everything else out?

Here's what happened. When Elijah got to the mountain, he waited for God to speak to him. All of a sudden there was a terrible blast—a reeeeally strong wind (tornado material)—so strong that the mountain started splitting. (True story. Read it yourself in 1 Kings 19:11-13.) Then there was an earthquake. Next (as if that wasn't enough action to last a year or so) there was a fire!

Wouldn't you think all these spectacular events meant God had spoken? (Stay with me, here, OK? We're getting to a really powerful part.)

Suddenly (after all that) there was the sound of a soft *whisper.* And when Elijah heard it, he *knew* it was the Lord.

Whoa!

Do you get it?

Most of the time when God speaks to you, it won't come in a powerful thundering voice, or a telegram from heaven, or through a message being written in the sky by a creative airplane pilot. (We *wish* it would happen that way. Things would sure seem a lot easier.) But

Reflecting . . .

1. Can you identify a specific time in your life that you felt God was speaking directly to you? Yes when I gave a $100 to my chvrch

2. What distractions need to be moved out of the way so you can learn to know the voice of God? Priondly Satan

3. Who can help keep you accountable so you don't fall into old habits? Pray for Help

most of the time when God speaks to you, his voice will come in a gentle whisper. And guess what? That whisper is going to come from *within*.

Know what that means? Again . . . it means when you learn the process of tuning everything else out (TV, radio, friends' voices) and tuning in to *his* voice, you're going to deepen your relationship with him.

Why? Because the more you know his voice, the more you'll respond to his voice. The better you know God, the more CONFIDENT a Christian you'll be.

A disciple who knows God's voice = a disciple who responds when God speaks = God working through your life to impact those around you!

A Christian who knows God's voice = a Christian who is *confident*. A confident Christian = one who will dare to take a stand in his school, at work, and in his non-Christian home.

How well do *you* know the voice of God?

Back to your question: How can I become closer to God? (I think you know the answer now.) What're you gonna do about it?

"I Always Wondered about That...."

Dear Susie:

I try to have faith in the Lord . . . but sometimes I just don't know! My friend has a very deep faith, and I want to be more like her. Any suggestions?

LEGAL, ALBERTA

Some people are just naturally more trusting. For others, faith is more difficult. Remember the apostle Thomas? He wanted to *see* the nail scars in the Lord's hands before he believed. Faith was hard for him.

But guess what? You don't need a *lot* of faith. Jesus tells us all we need is a small amount. In fact, he compares how much we need to the size of a mustard seed. Have you ever seen a mustard seed? It's about the size of a pin point! We're talking *microscopic!*

The fact that you're a Christian ▼

and have trusted God to forgive your sins proves you have faith. And yes, there *are* some things you can do to increase the little bit of faith you have:

1. Read your Bible consistently.

2. Pray daily.

If you're not used to doing these two things, I suggest setting a small goal for yourself. Start with something you *know* you can reach. For instance, say, "I'm going to read the Bible and pray for one minute every day." *Anyone* can spend *one minute* with God!

You'll easily meet your goal, and after a few weeks you'll probably want to increase it to two minutes, then three or five. But if you start out saying, "I'm going to spend an hour a day praying and reading the Bible," while we applaud your enthusiasm, you probably won't follow through. So be realistic and set a goal you know you can easily reach.

3. Surround yourself with other Christians.

4. Get involved in your local church.

If you're already doing all these things, watch your friend's life. What is she doing that you're not? Ask her. Close friends should be able to share their spiritual highs and lows. Ask her to pray with you about your concerns.

Dear Susie:

What is a "walk with God?" The adults at church are always telling us to read our Bibles every day. Where do I start? Would a devotional book help? Please explain this stuff to me.

MILWAUKIE, OREGON ▼

You're asking some *terrific* questions. First of all, get a Bible you can understand. There are several youth editions available at your local Christian bookstore. (This would be a gr-r-reat thing to ask for as a Christmas or birthday gift.) Spend some time browsing through the various ones on the market, then decide which one you like the best. If you have a Bible you're proud of and can understand, chances are you'll read it more often.

Yes, devotional books are also a good idea. And there are tons of fantastic ones written just for teens. Again, check your local Christian bookstore, and find one you like. But remember . . . a devotional book is not meant to *replace* your Bible. *No book* can take the place of God's Word. It's the *ultimate* devo book! I suggest reading your Bible in the morning and reading your devotional book in the evening.

What is a walk with God? It's a relationship. Just as you do specific things to maintain your friendships with guys and girls at your school, you'll want to do many of those same things to strengthen your friendship (or relationship) with your heavenly Father (talk with him, read his Word, keep him in charge of your life).

Dear Susie:

I'll be in high school next year, and my friend and I want to be an influence for God. What can a couple of ordinary girls do?

ELK CITY, OKLAHOMA

YES! *That's* the spirit! I'm excited that you're willing to "be the one!" You'll also want to be involved with "See You at the Pole"—a national movement of teens who dare to pray publicly one day out of the year at their school's flagpole. Last year over a million teens in junior high and high schools all over the United States were involved! Call 1-619-592-9200 for more information. In the meantime, keep reading for some more great ideas.

Dear Susie:

I've given my life to Christ, but I'm not sure he took me. I didn't have the tingly feeling everyone talks about. Did God accept me or not?

HOLLAND, MICHIGAN

You bet he did! He assures us in his Word that *everyone* who calls on his name *will* be saved (Joel 2:32)! He doesn't even mention feeling. Many people *do* feel tingly—or good—because they're just so happy that

God has saved them from a life of sin.

But perhaps you've always been a "good person." Maybe you weren't on drugs or anything . . . so when God saved you there wasn't a huge change in your life. (You were still forgiven of your sins, because the Bible says we're *all* born with sin—Romans 3:23.)

Just because you don't "feel" God doesn't mean you don't "have" him. That's where *faith* comes in. Memorize this, OK?

What is faith? It is the confident assurance that something we want is going to happen. It is the certainty that what we hope for is waiting for us, even though we cannot see it up ahead. (Hebrews 11:1-2, TLB*)*

You don't always *feel* the sun, but you believe it's still there, don't you? There are days you can't *feel* the wind, but you know the air still surrounds you. Same with God. Many times you won't *feel* him . . . but **trust,** BELIEVE, **know** that he's still with you.

Bottom line: He promised he'd never leave (John 14:18).

The Ghost of School Days ... Present

It's the first week of school and the halls are jammed as everyone races to their next class. But instead of being one of the herd on their way to biology, you've been given a gift. From a sitting position four feet above the densely crowded hallway—totally invisible—you sit like a teenage Ebenezer Scrooge, looking down on a world you normally inhabit.

No, this gift hasn't occurred so you'd discover the true meaning of Christmas. Instead, you're there to witness the daily competition.

Competition for what, you ask. Just watch and you'll see.

Right below you is Megan. She's talking to Christy, who's a grade ahead of her. Megan's trying to find out where the party is after the game this Friday.

Down the hall you spot Ray, a sophomore who's just made the var-

sity football team. He's walking a step behind three senior teammates who are laughing loudly and scoping out the babes as they pass by.

Just passing through the doorway is Lisa. She really "developed" over the summer and doesn't mind if guys

THE POPULARITY LADDER

notice. All through junior high she was shy and withdrawn; now she's turning heads. She's confident, and she makes eye contact with every cute guy who walks down the hall.

Different Names, Same Game

The game is called Popularity Pursuit. It happens in every hallway in every high school, junior high, and middle school in North America—no exceptions.

It's true, not everyone goes all-out in this game. Some only play when it's safe, others have nearly given up all together, a few aren't interested in playing—very few.

None of the people playing this game are bad, even the ones who are trying anything to succeed. They believe the secret to survival is moving up the popularity ladder as quickly as possible. If you asked them, they wouldn't tell you that getting to a "higher" group is their goal. But their actions tell a different story.

Even though you may be (unknowingly) playing this game at your school, let's assume for a minute you're not. You're "above" it. Either way, there's one thing you have in common with them: fairly early in the school year you'll maneuver into a group and will end up with a "sphere of influence." A circle of friends that:

- will influence you
- you will influence
- or both of the above

Some of these friends may be from good homes with stable families. But many will come from homes that are totally out of whack.

- Maybe a parent, brother, or sister is chemically dependent, and the family is trying to hide it.
- Perhaps a friend in your circle has been a victim of abuse.
- It's very common to have friends who have parents who are divorced or remarried.
- Maybe the family just doesn't spend any time together.

All these friends look normal on the outside, but *inside* most are carrying some hidden scars. I (Greg) was one of those kids.

Each of my parents was married three times before I was out of high school. They abused alcohol, and I even used to smoke dope with my dad. From my own experience—and from the hundreds of teens I've talked with—I know that when life throws you lemons you don't make lemonade. You build a protective shell around you to help cushion the blows. The longer people live within this shell, the thicker and harder it gets.

How does this relate to floating invisible in the hallway?

When people aren't given the chance to experience unconditional love from the safe confines of a family, they pursue popularity as a substitute. They unconsciously think, *Since*

I haven't received the love I know I need, I'll do what seems like the next best thing: find friends who will make me feel important and special.

Sadly, even many teens who come from loving homes choose to take that love for granted and start thinking Popularity Pursuit is a game they should play, too. Both junior high and high school have a way of convincing you it's the only game in town. After all, not being in the popular crowd doesn't always feel good.

What penetrated *my* shell (which had about six years of coating on it) was a number of Christians showing me what unconditional love was all about. Once I got a glimpse of how differently these folks treated me, I knew I wanted what they had.

What they had, of course, was a growing relationship with Jesus Christ. And they cared more about me than I did!

The Choice Is Yours

If you are tracking with what's been said, then you know you're faced with an important choice: Am I going to play Popularity Pursuit, or am I more concerned about being the best friend I can be in my sphere of influence?

If you're not sure you're able to quit playing Popularity Pursuit yet, we understand. But it's a game that never ends. There's always a "higher group" to pursue. Along the way, you forget about being a real friend to those who may need you.

What will it be?

Reflecting . . .

1 Why is Popularity Pursuit so tough *not* to play?

because every body wants to be notice

2 What type of people don't play this game?

I dont know

3 Any games *you've* been playing?

no

Choose Your Own Break

Right now is a gr-r-reat time to take a break.
Reward yourself for reading this far by:

1. Chewing a whole pack of grape Bubblicious

2. Eating a can of frozen lemonade without mixing it with water *(This is terrif. I promise! —Susie)*

3. Calling your mom or dad at work and reminding them how much you love 'em (Who knows? Maybe that'll make 'em so happy they'll treat you to McDonald's tonight!)

4. ~~Sending Susie some microwave popcorn (I'll love you forever! —Susie)~~

    4. Sending Greg some Upper Deck baseball cards.

    GET OUTTA HERE, GREG! I'm WRITING THIS PART.
    — SUSIE

Sticking with Friends Who Don't Want You

Dear Greg:

I have a friend who goes to my church and school. He used to be close to God. He acted and spoke like a Christian should. Lately, I've noticed that he's really falling away from God. He has started hanging out with the wrong crowd, cussing, and listening to music that's not right. But every time I try to talk to him he just makes fun of me and walks away. How can I help him?

ACTON, MAINE

First rule of friendships: You can't change someone who doesn't want to change. Even though you can see trouble on the horizon—and he can't—you've probably done all you can do, at least with him.

But you *can* do some detective work. Find out what's going on at home. When someone goes through a drastic behavior change, the trig-

ger is often a home life in turmoil. Here are some examples:

- If his dad used to be his hero and faithfully took the family to church, then abruptly left the family, you can be sure that will cause a son to question

55

whether this faith stuff is real—and whether it works.

- If his dad has become too preoccupied with work or other pursuits, your friend may be trying to get some attention.
- Sometimes a parent will be hurt by someone in the church and will rag on them at home or simply quit going. That can give a guy an excuse to "spread his wings" and try new things.

Try to find out from your pastor or other adults that know your friend's parents if everything is OK at home. Information like that may not change your friend, but at least you'll know *why* he's acting so different. Eventually, maybe you'll be able to talk to him about it—away from other "friends" at school—and he might open up.

Church Can Hurt Sometimes, Too!

Churches and youth groups aren't perfect. They're inhabited by forgiven sinners who still struggle with a selfish human nature. Perhaps one of the adult leaders really let your friend down or embarrassed him in front of a lot of people. That can trigger some angry actions. What better way to get back at the church than to start acting just the opposite of what it expects?

Talk to other kids or leaders in the group, and see if they can remember a time your friend could have been hurt. If so, try to get the one who offended him to apologize. That could clear the way for his return.

You may even want to ask your friend if *you* did anything that offended him. Hopefully not, but it can't hurt to ask.

The Inescapable Fact

Let's be honest. Being a Christian usually doesn't win you any points with the popular crowd. Some teens want desperately to be "in." They don't feel good about who they are, so they believe a change in groups will give them a new, "better" identity. They're even willing to brush aside a faith that once seemed so real, just to be "in."

It's next to impossible to confront someone by saying, "I think you're acting differently just so you can be more popular." They're either going to deny it or think you're jealous.

The best strategy is to do what you've already done. Talk to your friend about it, and find out what the scoop is. Consider taking another friend with you who feels the same—not to gang up on him, but to show your concern. If he refuses to listen, back off. Some people have to feed pigs before they come to their senses (see Luke 15 about a son who had to hit bottom before he could look up).

Keep the relationship open; continue being as good a friend as he lets you. Remember his birthday and Christmas—don't give up! Sooner or later he'll discover who his real friends are and will want to return (like the prodigal son). If he senses unconditional acceptance—and not judgment—you'll be the first one he turns to.

Dear brothers, if anyone has slipped away from God and no longer trusts the Lord and someone helps him understand the Truth again, that person who brings him back to God will have saved a wandering soul from death, bringing about the forgiveness of his many sins. (James 5:19-20, TLB)

Reflecting . . .

1 Write down the names of friends you know who once professed to be Christians, but aren't living it anymore. ~Clay

2 What could you or your youth group do to help these people get plugged in again to the Lord? bring him to church

3 Read Luke 15:11-32 and talk about why some people have to hit bottom before they look up. Discuss the reaction of the father and how you or your group could act the same way.

Real Friends . . .

- Offer to buy someone a soda or some popcorn.
- Help do a job that will go quicker with two people (e.g., raking leaves, picking up the house, shoveling out their closet, cleaning the gutters, folding ten loads of wash).
- Send a quick note (here are a few samples)

59

Clark-
Yo, Bud! Missed ya at youth group. Call me. Let's grab a Coke
Doug

Dear Jammy, I'm glad you're part of my world! You make me smile. Friends, Melissa

Tim-
Thanks for helping me with all those boxes last week. Let's go shoot some hoops this Saturday Greg

CHERYL - THANKS FOR MAKING ME THAT COCONUT CAKE SO I'D HAVE SOMETHING TO TAKE TO THE POTLUCK. WANNA GRAB SOME MEXICAN FOOD THIS WEEK?
— SUSIE

- Be available when there's a family emergency—like a death or divorce. (See chapter 15 for more help.)
- Let someone borrow one of your Christian tapes. Positive music can lift their spirits quickly as God's truth helps give them the right picture.
- Offer to pray for them if they need help beyond what you can give.
- Invite them to some of your family events. This is perfect for someone in a single-parent situation. They may need to see how a family with a loving mom and dad interacts with each other.
- Arrange your schedule so you can go to a friend's special event: recitals, choir concerts, computer chess tournaments, games, bar mitzvah, confirmation, whatever!
- Don't rag on their ideas all the time. There's nothing worse than having a friend that constantly has a better idea. Do stuff and try things they came up with—even if you think your idea is better.
- Tell the truth. That is:

1. If you did something wrong, admit it and apologize.
2. If they did something good (no matter how small), tell them.
3. If they did well in school, congratulate them.
4. If they got a present that's cool, don't ignore it or get jealous—*tell* them it's cool.
5. If they got the courage to call that girl they've waited three months to call, mention that you admire it.
6. If their clothes look good, dish out a compliment.
7. If you notice them doing something nice for someone else, let them know you saw it and you're glad you're their friend. (OK, that's a little syrupy for guys, but sometimes you don't have say it—sometimes a look says it all.)
8. If they're messing up their life with alcohol, drugs, or an unhealthy relationship, find the right time and let them know you care about them too much to let this continue without saying something. Don't give ultimatums, and don't hit the road just because your friend has started something destructive. That's the time friends need you the most!

- Remember special events: birthdays, spiritual birthdays, graduations, their 6,000th day on earth, etc.
- Buy them a pet (a small cat or dog will be a constant reminder of your friendship).

60

But better check with their folks first. If this is too expensive, consider a stuffed animal (girls only).

- Come to their defense. If a friend is in trouble, wrongly accused, or just needs another person to be with them when they're facing some consequences, be the one to stand with them.

- Thank them for things they've done for you. Don't ever assume people know you're thankful—verbalize it.

- Real friends are optimistic! Don't dwell on the negative or always be the one to point out what could go wrong. If you look for the good, you'll often find it.

Reflecting . . .

1 List three things friends have done for *you* in the past two months.

Zach
Jhon
Aron

2 What is some neat stuff you've done for others to demonstrate your friendship?

Thanking the more then once

CHAPTER 14

True Colors

I (Susie) used to teach high-school speech and drama. Because of the electives I taught, I generally had only juniors and seniors. Once in a while a sophomore would sneak in, but not very often.

This particular year, however, Aaron had just moved to our town from out-of-state, and because he'd done a little acting at his old school, they placed him in our drama class as a sophomore.

Aaron was different. Well, to be blunt, he was a geek. A total geek! It was the first of the year, and I was placing students in front of the class for quick improvisations to get them comfortable being in front of a group.

I hadn't placed Aaron in front of the class yet because he was having enough trouble *in* the class. He was always doing something really

dorky, and the others never missed an opportunity to rag on him.

Now I had certain rules in my class. One of those rules was to maintain a positive attitude and not be critical of anyone's performance. (It's hard enough getting in front of

63

a group, right? We don't need to be razzed once we're up there. We need affirmation and support.)

As a result, students were pretty careful about what they said within my hearing range. What I couldn't control, of course, was the way they treated Aaron between classes.

A week went by, and I still hadn't placed him in front of the class. I was really worried about it. I knew I had to give him a grade. He *had* to get in front of the group eventually, but I felt sorry for him. I didn't want the others to make fun of him.

A few more days passed, and I finally got an idea. I'd heard Tiffani talk about her youth group and some of the fun stuff they had planned. She seemed to have her act together. If she was really a Christian (like she claimed), shouldn't I be able to count on her to act in an improv with Aaron without cutting him down?

And I thought of Tom. The quarterback for our high-school football team. He was a Christian. He even carried his Bible to school. Kids respected him. He was excited about his relationship with the Lord. He virtually wore it to school every day.

The time had finally come for Tom and Tiffani's true colors to shine through. The next day I called Aaron's name, along with Tom and Tiffani. I gave them an improv setup.

Tom began. He was such a studmuffin that *anything* he said or did was quickly accepted. He was just cool, you know? Then Tiff chimed in. She was head cheerleader. Cute. Popular. Charming little giggle.

Then Aaron began acting . . . and totally blew it. He was as geeky on stage as he was off. I could feel the tension in the air. Students were half-poised in their desks ready to blurt out all kinds of criticism— even at the expense of getting in trouble with me, the teach.

I could just imagine their thoughts:

Aaron, you're such a dork-brain! Why don't you sign up for a class with all the other sophomores?

Oh, man!

What a doofus!

Get him off! The guy's a jerk.

It happened in just a split second . . . he moved *so* quickly! I was absolutely stunned. Right before those thoughts had a chance to become verbalized, big, muscular, athletic Tom threw his arms around Aaron's waist and hurled him over his shoulders like a huge sack of potatoes. Then he swung him around, patted him on the back, and said, laughing, "Aaron, you're my buddy. You are *my* pal!"

He did all this while walking out the front door of my classroom with Tiff following. And in that split second I grabbed the opportunity to call three more students to the front and began the next improv.

By the time Tom, Tiff, and Aaron came in through the back door and took their seats, the class's attention was already focused on another improv with different kids.

Wow!

My heart leapt.

I can't help but believe that's exactly what Jesus would have done. He would have immediately taken the attention off Aaron and the geeky thing he did and placed it on himself. Then he would have separated Aaron from the crowd so he wouldn't feel the criticism.

That's exactly what he did with the woman caught in adultery, wasn't it? He took the attention off her and separated the crowd. Then he affirmed her. (See John 8:1-11.)

"Aaron, you're my buddy. You are *my* pal!" Tom was being Jesus to Aaron. I'm convinced he did *exactly* what our Father God would have done.

We had an hour for open-campus lunch. (Students were allowed to leave the school grounds and return an hour later.) I saw Tiffani, a senior, driving down the crowded street in front of the school with Aaron in the passenger seat. A *senior cheerleader* was taking a *sophomore geek* out to lunch!

I knew she would take some

razzing when she returned. Sure enough, I heard it during hall duty. "Hey, Tiff! What's the deal? You got the hots for *Aaron?*"

"Yeah. We saw you guys going out to lunch!"

"Hey, Tiff, you two *going* together?"

Tiff simply laughed and held her head high. She was being Jesus to Aaron. I'm convinced that's exactly what God would have done.

Tiff and Tom were both secure. Confident. They were so excited about their relationship with Christ they couldn't help but reach out to others. But they didn't just reach out to the popular kids. Popular kids are *easy* to love. These two cared enough to reach out to kids who ate alone. Students who *weren't* cool. They risked their own reputation to be Jesus to those who needed him.

How were they so confident? How can I be more confident like that?

KEY: The closer you grow to Christ, the more confident you become. The more you fall in love with Jesus, the more you can't help but love others.

See, Jesus knows you better than anyone in the entire world. Yet he also *loves* you! He knows the parts of *you* that are geeky, too. He knows, because he knows *everything,* and you just can't hide stuff from God. But even though he sees the bad, the negative, and the geeky in you, he's madly in love with you. Crazy about you. So overwhelmed by you that he gave his *life* . . . just for you!

When you spend quality time in the Bible, you can't help but deepen your relationship. And the more you talk with him and listen to what he says, the closer your relationship becomes.

The closer you grow to Christ, ● the more *confident* you become. You begin to place your security in him. That means you allow *Jesus* to be your source of happiness and fulfillment instead of boyfriends, girlfriends, grades, sports achievements, or even popularity. Because Jesus becomes the very *center* of your life, everything takes on a new perspective. It becomes important to you to reach out. To love others. To be Jesus to your world.

—Reflecting . . .—

1 List three different ways you can reach out to friends in the next three weeks. (Invite them to youth group, send a cool note, make a phone call, go out for a diet Coke float, etc.)

- inviting them to crossover
- be a friend
- tell them I'm there for them

2 Spend at least three minutes each day for the next three weeks praying for the people on your list.

3 Tell God you want *him* to be your source of security, happiness, and fulfillment instead of _____ school _____.

(you fill it in)

When Friends Are Hurting

Jeff's dad left last weekend and said he wasn't coming back.

Merideth's grandma is in the hospital and will die any day.

Aaron's girlfriend, Laura, called him at home last night saying she wanted to break up with him. They'd been going together for seven months. He's devastated.

Becky tried out for rally in front of the whole school. She was voted down even though she was better than some of the other, more popular girls.

Thomas just learned that his younger brother has leukemia.

Laurie broke down crying in health class. When you talked to her later, she told you her uncle used to molest her.

Scott's dad comes home drunk nearly every night. Last night he started to get physical with Scott and his brothers.

Stuff Happens

This can be a mixed-up world sometimes. While a few people go through their teen years without a

67

major crisis, most don't. The first to hear when something goes haywire is usually a best friend.

When things go wrong, some people can hide it. They put on a normal face, say, "It'll be all right," and try to change the subject. Inside, though, they're in major hurt. Their stomach is twisting, they have a million questions, and they don't think anyone understands what they're going through.

What **you** should do depends on how serious the problem is. If their dog died, they basically just need time to recover. (Pets can really get attached to their owners!) But when a parent or a sibling is abusing alcohol, the whole family suffers, and it's an ongoing problem that won't get better without help.

How do you help? After all, you're not a professional counselor.

That's probably the first lesson you should learn. Some problems, like those on the list below, are too big for you to handle alone. The best thing you can do is find a teacher, counselor, youth leader, pastor—or maybe even one of your parents—to see if they can go to the next level of care for the hurting person.

Problems You Should Not Try to Tackle Alone

- If a friend is in trouble with the law

- If the person needs medical help
- If someone talks about hurting someone else or about suicide
- If your friend is using drugs or alcohol
- If the person has been (or is being) sexually, physically, or emotionally abused
- If your friend seems emotionally unable to handle the situation they're in

The Smaller Stuff

Minor crises your friends face usually just need a listening ear sandwiched between some good questions. Usually, however, when a friend tells us about a problem, our first urge is to try to fix it. Our buddy is hurting, and we want the hurt to stop. Fight the urge to give advice. Instead, ask questions that will help your friend know what the hurt is:

- **Tell me how you feel.** (Pause, wait for answer.) **Anything else?** (Don't say, "I know how you feel." Especially if you've never experienced what they're going through. Even if you have, it's not time to talk yet.)
- **What hurts the most?**
- **Have you talked to anyone else? What did they say? What do you think about what they said?**

- **Is there anything you could have done to prevent this from happening?**
- **What can you do to make the situation better?**
- **Have you prayed about it?** (If not, pray right then.)

That line of questioning alone will lead many conversations to a close. You've given your friend a chance to express their hurt and helped them find out if it was their fault. You've helped them get perspective on the situation. When they come to the realization that they couldn't have done anything to prevent it, that usually will bring some measure of comfort. (Remember, this is for *small* problems.)

If they ask for your advice after these questions, now may be the time. Sometimes people *do* need a different angle on the situation, so giving your opinion can really help. But try to wait until they ask for it.

The Big Stuff

When a major crisis hits, some of the above questions may help, but usually the pain is too intense. Your friend just needs you to be there to listen in case they need to talk. Proverbs is right when it says, "A friend loves at all times, and a brother is born for adversity" (Proverbs 17:17). Big problems faced together can cement a friendship for a

lifetime. Obviously that's not the goal, it's just the natural result. So don't shy away from being the first one there when bad times hit.

Here are a few other ideas:

First, listen to your friend, but don't play "Mr. Answerman." Don't walk into the room with false cheerfulness, and don't offer wisdom, advice, and a bunch of Bible verses. Try not to worry about not being sure what to say or do—that's natural. In fact, it's probably best not to say much at all. Just be there with the grieving person and listen.

Second, share your heart—not your mind. A friend who has lost someone—through death *or* divorce—has usually heard the answers from other caring friends and family. Where they're hurting the most is in their heart. So intellectual answers really won't help much. Ask them to have lunch or dinner with you. Ask them to see a movie. Just be a friend.

Here are some other things to keep in mind . . .

In Divorce

- Realize that divorce is like death. Though divorce is common today, it doesn't make the pain easier to bear. People often receive cards and flowers when someone dies. Your friend might also appreciate a note or card just saying that you care.

- Listen to the same story again and again . . . as many times as they need to share it.
- Continue to hang out with them at school. They don't have leprosy, they're just hurting. Keep your house open to them, too.
- If they seem extremely upset, encourage them to talk to your pastor, school counselor, or your own parents.
- Help them get involved in other activities. Maybe you have a hobby and could include them, even if it's only for a little while.
- Offer to help them if they're having problems with their schoolwork. When a person is grieving, it's hard to concentrate on history, math . . . even P.E.
- Keep an open mind, and don't make negative comments about either of their parents. This may help them realize they don't have to take sides. Recovery will be easier if they keep communication open with both parents.

In Death

- Encourage them to talk. It's helpful for the grieving person to put their feelings into words. ▼

- Ask them if they want you to go with them to view the body at the funeral home. For some people this is a very private moment to share only with family members, but others appreciate having a friend with them.
- Attend the funeral. Your presence will show your support and your love.
- Do something practical to help the family, like taking food to their home.
- Allow your friend to cry when they need to. Don't be embarrassed by deep emotion.
- Give them time to grieve. The grief process takes months, even years, to pass through. Don't expect them to bounce back immediately from their pain.
- Pray for them. Ask God to give you ideas to help them.

Other Ideas

- Continue to include them in activities. Their world has fallen apart. If they stay involved in some of their regular activities, it can help them feel secure.
- Don't be afraid to touch someone who's hurting. A hand on the shoulder can communicate more strongly than words.
- As you listen to them talk,

don't try to top their story with one of your own.

- Often, grieving people say things they don't really mean. Don't be easily offended at what they may say. Continue to stand by them and support them even when it gets rough.
- If they ask for your opinion or advice, give it. Otherwise, keep quiet.
- Get them involved in strenuous physical activities. Getting lots of physical exercise often helps a person deal with emotional pressure.
- Continue to pray for them and their entire family. Ask God to comfort and strengthen them.

We've talked about how to be a better friend in good times and bad. Now we're going to turn the corner and start dealing directly with introducing your Best Friend in heaven to your best friend on earth. As you'll see in the next chapter, that's sometimes easier said than done.

Reflecting . . .

1 When you are hurting with small stuff, how do *you* want to be comforted? How about the big stuff? *With small stuf I want them to be sad with me & To comfort me*

2 Can you think of a friend who is hurting right now? *no*

3 What specifically can you do to reach out to him or her?

"The Invisible Man Is My Best Friend!"

Raise your hand if Jesus Christ is your best friend.

OK, now raise your hand if you've ever seen Jesus Christ.

Hmmmm.

The questions that would come to my mind if I was Joe non-Christian are:

"So, you're seeing a whole team of psychiatrists, aren't you?"

"What's it like to spend time in padded cells?"

"Are those men in white coats very friendly?"

Those are fair questions to ask, too . . . IF you've never seen him at work in your life and in the lives of others.

Even if you know for 100 percent proof positive that Jesus Christ is alive and well and living in your heart, that often doesn't make it any easier to explain. It's . . . unnatural ▼

to talk about Someone you can never introduce face-to-face in this life. Here's a sample conversation:

"I'd like you to turn your life over to someone you can't see," you tell your best friend. "His name is Jesus Christ. He lived two thou-

73

sand years ago here on earth, but he's really been alive since the beginning of time . . . which is a very long time. Probably higher than I could count

"Anyway, he's really cool because he loves you to death. In fact, he died on a cross to pay the penalty for your sins. You know—those things we do because we're humans. It's our nature to be selfish and mess up. We can't help it. He died for that, too!

"Anyway, if you ask him for forgiveness and accept him into your heart . . . huh? . . . No, a miniature Jewish guy with a white robe and a beard doesn't actually go into your heart, or your stomach for that matter—he's a Spirit. He's invisible. But I know he comes into your life because he came into mine. Let me finish.

"Once you believe that he died on a cross and rose from the dead, you have eternal life! That means when you die, you don't go to hell. Hell's a place with lots of hot fire and millions of bad people like Hitler. Boy, are they getting their just deserts now! Huh? No, I don't know where it is, and I've never seen it, but the Bible says it's a real place.

"The Bible? Oh, didn't I tell you about the Bible? Well, here's one. Yeah, it's kinda big, and there aren't a lot of pictures, but this Book explains everything about God and Moses and Jesus and sin and faith and heaven and hell.

"Who's Moses? Well, he's a guy in the Old Testament. You know, Charlton Heston. Like in The Ten Commandments. You've seen that movie, haven't you? He's not important right now anyway. What's really important is what you're going to do with Jesus Christ. That's the big issue.

"What does it all mean to me? Well, it means I'm going to heaven, which is cool. It means I go to church every Sunday and on Wednesday nights, which is sometimes cool. It means that when I pray, I know he's listening, and I can go to him whenever I need help or when I'm lonely. Doesn't he sound like a good friend to have?

"What do you mean you want to see him first? You can't see him. You have to believe by faith that he's there.

"No, it's not like mind over matter. It's a thing called faith. I know he's there. I've felt him. I've seen my prayers answered! Now do you want to accept him into your heart, or not?"

Invisible Man, Impossible Task

Thankfully, that type of conversation doesn't happen too often. In fact, I'm sure one like that has *never* happened. If a friend was thinking logically, though, it certainly could come close.

For most of us, the dilemma isn't having someone we can't see as a best friend . . . it's knowing how to explain it! Before we get to the parts on how to explain it, let's talk about the first part: having a best friend named Jesus.

First, let me ask you, *is* he your best friend? He sure *wants* to be! He also wants to be LORD of your life. That means he wants you to allow him to call the shots in every area. He not only wants to be your number-one best friend, he wants to be NUMBER ONE.

For most of us, that's a process. You don't wake up one day and allow him to take complete control for the rest of your life. He knows that, so all he asks for is a heart-attitude that wants to try to let him run the show, but is not afraid to admit it when you fail.

A "heart-attitude" is your motivation from the inside to love him and serve him. While you can maybe fool everyone else, you can't fool yourself—or God.

Here's how you can tell where your attitude is.

If you grew up going to church, you likely went because your parents took you. But as you hit the teenage years, you have an important decision to make: *Do I* ▼

believe all this stuff about God and Jesus because my parents believe it, or because I know it's true? Is my faith mine, or is it someone else's?

To be more specific, ask yourself this question: *Have I made a "lifetime identity decision" to follow and obey Jesus Christ for the rest of my life? That is, have I decided that all this Christian stuff is true, and there's no room in my life to ever turn away from it?*

Heavy-duty choice, huh?

But until you've come to the place in your own heart and mind where you can say, "Yes, I have made a lifetime identity choice to follow Christ," your friendship with Jesus will stay on an acquaintance level. If that's the case, tell me—would you bother risking a conversation like the fictional one a couple of pages ago for someone who's just an acquaintance?

I wouldn't! I'd keep quiet about this guy, Jesus, until I was really certain.

And if you're not sure yet, that may be the best thing to do. But keep asking questions and observing other Christians who have made that choice. Take your time, and don't think that just because you aren't best friends with Jesus Christ now you never will be. It takes time to develop a best friendship. You just need more time, that's all.

If you didn't grow up going to church, but became a Christian later in life, trusting Christ as your Savior was probably that lifetime identity choice. You lived your life away from him, now you know him . . . the difference between the two lives is obvious. "Sure," you say. "He's my best friend. No doubt!"

Keeping Him Best Friend

Once you start holding on to Jesus Christ as your LORD (first) and best friend (second), it's tough sometimes to keep a grip on him. There are hundreds of distractions—and one dirty guy who wants you to let go. Why? Well, here's another conversation that makes it obvious.

"Hi, Staci, I've been wanting to introduce you to my best friend, Jesus, for a long time.

"Where did he go?

"Oh NO, I forgot! I let go of his hand last month. Well, I guess I'll have to introduce him to you later. Bye."

The distractions that cause us to let go of Jesus' hand are everywhere. They scream at us for our time and attention:

- school activities
- a guy or girlfriend
- TV, music, and movies
- magazines and books (maybe even this one!)
- homework
- a job
- volunteer work
- late nights and early mornings
- other friends we can see a little better than Jesus
- maybe even church activities

All of these and more keep us so busy sometimes that we forget about Jesus (you know, the one we can't see).

And then there's this other guy who *really* hates us: Satan. He will do absolutely anything and everything to keep us from spending time with Jesus. He knows that if he can slowly keep us occupied with "things"—even *Christian* things—then he can distract us from our most important task: letting others know by our life and our words that Jesus Christ is right beside us and offers everyone eternal life.

Satan is committed to undercutting our best friendship with Jesus every day, every hour, every minute. He knows what a Christian with a close relationship with Jesus can do . . . and he doesn't want that at all!

We've talked about having a close relationship with Christ in chapter 7. Once you've made that lifetime identity choice to stick with Christ, there's one more major thing to keep in mind as you share your faith.

(That was a transitional sentence to set up the next chapter. Keep reading.)

～～～～ Reflecting . . . ～～～～

1 Is it tough to make a lifetime identity choice to follow Christ in your teen years?

yah

2 How does that choice relate to sharing your faith?

dont know

3 If you haven't made that choice, what is holding you back?

The Real Goal

You've stuck with us this far. Great work! That tells us you're really serious about being the best friend you can be.

Hopefully, you've caught one theme throughout the book: All of your friends are valuable; they're too valuable to be looked on as *projects,* instead of real *people.*

Not every friend will be ready to become a Christian just because you're ready for them to dive into it. Remember, the goal isn't to be the one to lead someone to Christ; the goal is to be available to God to move them one or two notches closer to understanding the depth of God's love for them. *He* does the saving; *he* gets the credit. We didn't die for them, we only tell them about someone who did.

And speaking of taking the credit . . . pride is a funny thing with Christians. We struggle with it like every-

one else. Spiritual pride might be the worst. It's the feeling that "I'm higher up, more spiritually mature, or God loves me more because I'm sharing my faith." If that's your goal, God won't honor your efforts. Your heart's prayer needs to be this each day:

Father God, this day I want to take my eyes off myself and put them on someone who needs to know your love. Give me an opportunity to be the best friend I can be. Use me, and don't let me take the credit for anything good that happens. You alone deserve the credit. Amen.

If you can start every day with those words, there is NO LIMIT as to how much God will use you during your teenage years. You'll understand—like few adults do—the real reason God put you here on this planet: There's a life-and-death mission to accomplish. The time is short. Before you know it, college and routine adulthood will be the norm for your life. Though for some of your friends the shell around their heart is already too hard, most are more open to the gospel during these years than they will be at any other time in their life. Especially when it comes from a good friend.

We've both talked to dozens of kids who admitted they wasted their high-school years; there were so many hurting people who needed them, but they were too busy and too unconcerned. Don't be one of these people.

Enjoy your teenage years; be involved in a lot of different things; but as you go, don't forget the friends God has placed around you. Remember . . .

The Lord is not slow in keeping his promise, as some understand slowness. He is patient with you, not wanting anyone to perish, but everyone to come to repentance. (2 Peter 3:9)

Reflecting . . .

1 How can spiritual pride damage your relationship with others? With Christ?

You don't give him credit

2 Why is it tempting to take the credit when God uses you to help others?

It seems like you did a lot of it

3 How can you keep from allowing this to happen?

Pray about it

How to Be a Tool

Forget about saving *anyone*. Remember, it's God's responsibility. *He* does the saving; *we're* just the tool.

Have you ever thought a rake could have fun? (If you have, you're weird.) Think about it. A rake is most useful when it's being used for what it was created for.

Same with you.

You were created to know God, love him, and to be available as a tool in his hand. It's an absolute kick to know God's used you for something. He doesn't even care if it's something *we think* is itty-bitty. He's excited for the chance to let us in on what he's doing. Ain't no better feeling!

I don't know too many people whose goal is to be pegged a religious nut. So if Jesus Christ really is your best friend, how do you give him away without looking like one? ▼

Learn How to Talk to People

Most Christian teens know *what* to say; they just don't know *how* to say it. God doesn't want you to get on the school PA and preach. He just wants you to be ready (see 1 Peter 3:15). Sure, it's important to know

HEAVENLY TOOL BOX

81

some of the facts about Jesus, but if you're too scared to tell anyone, what good will the facts do them?

The only way to get better at something is to practice (that's why we've included some special practice situations for you in chapter 23—starting on page 103). Sit down with your dad, mom, a Christian friend, the mirror—anything—and put into words the important stuff about Christ. This may be "just the facts." Or it may be your own story of how Christ has worked in your life. (We'll teach you how to do that, too, in chapters 26 and 27—pages 115 and 121.)

Learn How to Care for People

What gets people's attention is GENUINE CONCERN. It doesn't matter what Hollywood tells us—it's not sissy to show someone they're important. When a friend needs a friend, be the first one there. Listen, help with homework, buy a shake—BE *WITH* THEM. (See chapter 13 for our list of ideas—page 59.)

Important fact: When someone faces bad times, it can do one of two things to them: (1) It causes them to build a shell around their heart so they'll be numbed to the pain (in case it happens again), or (2) it encourages them to find answers so they can make sense out of it. This is where you come in.

If someone's not there with the answers when they're ready to hear them, your friend will build a shell. Though many teens your age already have a shell as thick as an adult's, most are still forming their shells. Maybe you'll be the one to offer some real medicine for their hurt before the shell gets too thick.

Learn How to Pray for People

There's "spiritual junk" happening all around you. If you're in a public school, you know exactly what I mean. The only way to really fight against these forces is to pray. (Grab a Bible and read Ephesians 6:10-18.)

You may find that some friends who couldn't give a rip about God today are suddenly open to him after you've spent some time praying that Satan would take a hike. (Kinda neat that Christ—who's living inside you—is this powerful, huh?)

Reflecting . . .

1 What do you think is the toughest part about sharing your faith?

Do You Have a Heart?

God smiles when we reach out to others. But to reach out we have to really care. Do *you* have a genuine burden for those around you who don't know Christ? Check your caring quotient with our heart-for-others quiz.

1. Eddie comes to school every Monday morning still halfway bombed from the night before. You . . .

    a. ignore him. Maybe someday he'll learn his lesson.

    b. speak to him. "Hi, Eddie. I think we're having a test in Mrs. Maffett's class today."

    c. invite him to church. "Hey, Eddie, wanna come to 'Power Hour' this Wednesday with me? It's our weekly youth meeting, and you might think it sounds like a

drag, but it's really a lot of fun. Try it just once, and I'll never hassle you again. But if you turn me down I'm gonna keep on ya every now and then, because I really

8
3

want you to give it a shot. Can I pick you up?"

d. quietly tell the vice-principal Eddie's bombed again.

2. There's a new student in your English class. You . . .

a. introduce yourself and ask if she wants to have lunch with you and your friends.

b. tell a few kids from your church to make her feel welcome.

c. are too caught up with your own friends to even notice her.

d. feel for her because you know what it's like to be new, but don't have the courage to do anything about it.

3. Someone you know (not super well, but well enough to say hi to in the halls because you have some classes together) has just been dumped by her boyfriend. You . . .

a. silently breathe a prayer for her.

b. send a note telling her that you care.

c. make it a point to speak with her: "Listen, I'm really sorry about what you're going through. If you need a Coke it's my treat, OK?"

d. note that it's none of your business and steer clear.

4. Your youth group has just had an incredible Burger Bash. About a hundred kids showed up, and everyone's excited about what God is doing in the lives of your friends. It's almost eleven-thirty, and you have to be home by midnight. The gym's a mess. Everyone except your youth minister and a couple of adults are still just hanging around. You . . .

a. leave immediately so you won't be late getting home.

b. tell a few of the seventh graders they need to stay and help clean the place up.

c. thank the adults for the great party and head home.

d. call your folks and explain that the gym looks like a hurricane hit it. Then you ask permission to stay a little later to help clean up.

5. The star forward for your school's basketball team has just been hospitalized for knee surgery. He'll be out the rest of the season. You . . .

a. stop by the hospital and let him know you care.

b. ignore the entire situation. After all, you're in the band. . . . He doesn't really care about *you,* so why should *you* care about *him?*

c. just send him a funny card

because hospitals give you the willies.

d. ask your youth minister to visit him.

6. Sara has been hanging around some different kids at school. Everyone knows they have bad reputations. She's missed a few Wednesday night youth meetings, and you can't even remember the last time she was in Sunday school. You . . .

a. think she's probably getting what she deserves hanging around jerks like that.

b. call your youth minister and share your concern with him.

c. call Sara and tell her if she knows what's good for her, she'll get back in church.

d. make a point to catch her in the cafeteria and let her know she's missed. You also offer to give her a ride for this week's meeting and tell her you'll call tonight to see if she's coming.

7. There's a kid at your school who's obviously from a very poor family. He always wears the same pair of jeans and only has a few T-shirts. His tennis shoes are *not* the cool kind, and they even have a hole in the bottom. You . . .

a. ask your parents if you can go through the family's

clothes and pull out stuff that might fit him. Then you take it to the school counselor and ask him to make sure it gets to him in a non-embarrassing manner.

b. think, *If his dad would get a decent job maybe he wouldn't have to look like such a dorknoid!*

c. leave an anonymous note on his locker with the address of Goodwill on it.

d. ask your youth minister if your group can collect some money or clothing for the family.

8. Your youth leader has just announced the youth trip for spring break. This year you're going on a short-term, inner-city mission trip out of state. It will cost approximately two hundred dollars. You . . .

a. join the others with ideas for money-raising projects.

b. feel extremely disappointed. After all, you'd been saving and hoping for a ski trip during spring break.

c. decide not to go since some seniors have invited you to go camping with them.

d. realize that even though this may not be as fun as skiing, it will probably be a life-changing experience, so you display a positive attitude.

9. Your Sunday school teacher is really boring. You . . .

   a. quit going to Sunday school.

   b. hang around for a while after class and ask if you can help implement some new ideas for part of the class time, like: playing a Christian music video for the first five minutes of class; taking five minutes at the end of class to ask each member what's going on in their lives; sharing prayer requests and answers; "interviewing" an older church member for five minutes each week so the class can get to know more people in the congregation.

   c. complain to your youth minister that if he doesn't do something soon, the entire class is going to fall apart.

   d. switch churches.

10. Your youth group is small, and when your youth leader is out of town, things seem to fall apart until he returns. When he leaves on vacation this summer you'll . . .

   a. volunteer to lead a two-week Bible study to keep things running consistently.

   b. open your home for fun,

games, refreshments, and videos a few times while he's gone, so kids will stay tuned in to church activities.

   c. look forward to a nice break from having to go to church all the time.

   d. sit around and complain with your friends that there's nothing to do.

Scoring

Add your points according to the chart below.

1. A = 0, B = 1, C = 2, D = 0
2. A = 2, B = 1, C = 0, D = 0
3. A = 1, B = 2, C = 3, D = 0
4. A = 0, B = 0, C = 1, D = 2
5. A = 3, B = 0, C = 2, D = 1
6. A = 0, B = 1, C = 0, D = 2
7. A = 3, B = 0, C = 0, D = 2
8. A = 1, B = 0, C = 0, D = 1
9. A = 0, B = 2, C = 0, D = 0
10. A = 2, B = 2, C = 0, D = 0

19–22 You've Got a Heart for Others!

You really care about those around you and have developed some terrific skills for reaching out. Congrats! You're striving to be Jesus to your world.

10–18 You've Got a Heart That *Wants* to Care for Others!

You definitely care about people, but sometimes you're afraid to reach out. You feel a little insecure about letting others know you care. But guess what? You're headed in the right direction. Increase your time spent with the Lord, and ask him to increase your confidence.

5–9 Your Heart's Beating, But Not for Others

Whoa! Quit thinking about yourself so much, and start focusing on the needs of those around you. Ask your youth pastor (or trusted adult friend) to help you become more concerned about the world around you. Strive to come up with some specific ideas together that will help turn your heart around.

0–4 Do You Even Have a Heart?

Wowsers! Sure am glad you have this book . . . are you really *reading* it, though? From your response you've indicated that you don't give a rip about others. Is that really true, or did you just wanna come in last to be funny? Ask your parents or youth minister for suggestions on becoming more caring. Then, seek God's forgiveness for being so coldhearted. You're special! God dreams B-I-G for you . . . let him warm your heart.

Boring Barry: The Kid without a Story

Can God Really Use Someone Who's Made Good Choices?

The butterflies are starting to kick in—BIG TIME. Scanning the room, taking a quick count, whoaaa, there's over forty people here!

Games and songs are almost over. I can't believe I let Steve talk me into doing this! There's the glance and the wink. Please God, don't let my voice crack.

"I've asked Barry to give his testimony at youth group tonight before we close. I've known him for about two years, and I think he's got some important things to share. Now, he's probably a little nervous, so let's give him a hand as he comes up."

"Uh . . . hello. My name's Barry. Oh . . . uh, I guess you already knew that."

Great start, dweeb face.

"You're probably wondering why Steve asked me to speak tonight. Um, me too!"

All right! That got a few laughs!

"Most of you have seen me around here for a long time. I just

UMM...

turned fourteen, and next year I'll be starting my freshman year at South."

High school, at last!!

"He wanted me to say some things about myself. Here goes.

"Well . . . I've never taken drugs or been to any drinking parties before. To be honest, I probably wouldn't even know how to act if I went to one."

That's really impressive, Barry. Wow them some more.

"Girls and I get along pretty good. I like being friends for a while before I start talking to them on the phone. They sure know how to talk!"

. . . and talk, and talk, and talk . . .

"After a couple months, if our personalities fit, we'd maybe spend time together watching basketball games after school. I'm kinda glad things never get too serious though; I'm not really ready for something long-term."

Though more short-term stuff wouldn't be so bad.

"My parents are still married to each other. Um, they tell us kids they'll *never* get divorced. Though they've faced some pretty tough times, like last summer when my dad lost his job, I can tell by the way they treat each other—they're committed. I'm real thankful for my parents. I love them a lot."

Now you're rolling.

"Ever since I can remember I've

gone to church. I guess you can say I was raised here. I remember when I was six, my mom asked me if I wanted to ask Jesus to come into my heart. I said yes. So we prayed, and I asked him in.

"I try to pray pretty much every day. I read my Bible about every other day. I'm hoping to do better once summer baseball is over.

"Um . . . I love coming to youth group. Steve's crazy, and, uh, a lot of you have really stuck with me. Especially after my grandma died last Christmas. I really felt your prayers."

These people really are my friends!

"Middle school has a lot of pressures. You know. But I've always known a Christian has to take a stand sooner or later. I decided for me it'd be sooner.

"I still make lots of mistakes. Like I'm always bashing on my little brother. He deserves it most of the time, though."

I'm glad I don't have an older brother who bashes on me!

"I'm looking forward to high school because people, I think, know the kind of person I am. I don't get asked anymore to go to parties. I think they think I'm the goody-goody type."

At least that's one pressure I won't have to deal with again—for a while anyway.

"I try to be friendly to everyone so they'll ask me why I'm so happy. Though it's tough to do, I really believe it's important to let others know how much Jesus means to me. Um, I have a lot of room to get better here. After all, no one wants to go so overboard that they lose friends! But some kids at our school, you know who I'm talking about, really need Jesus bad."

Actually, just like the rest of us!

"That's about all I have to say. Thanks for being here when I need you.

"Uh . . . Steve?"

Thank you, Jesus, it's over!

Sound boring? Not to us.

Hundreds of thousands of kids ● could give a testimony just like Barry's, but you don't ever see a four-page magazine spread on them, do you?

Though you may not have "a real conversion story," it doesn't mean you don't have anything to say. Never experiencing the "other side" is nothing to be ashamed of.

Many think it's more exciting to hear someone who's been radically changed. It is exciting, but God and we think it's just as awesome to *grow up* trying to follow Christ.

Wanna hear about Susie's real-life, incredibly dramatic story about how she became a Christian? Hey, flip the page—I wouldn't keep you waiting.

You Don't Have to Be on Drugs or Sleep Around to Have a Testimony

I was brought up in a Christian home. Two loving parents. A neat dog. Piano lessons. Good-looking older bro. Our home was pretty close to perfect. I had *friends* who struggled with getting yelled at, having alcohol abuse in the home, and never hearing "I love you." But, personally, I couldn't relate.

I *listened* and sympathized . . . but could never truthfully say, "I understand" or, "I know what you're going through." As a result, I began to wonder if I even *had* a testimony. I mean I couldn't ever say, "I've been abused, but God has given me the strength to survive." Or, "I've messed with pot . . . snorted a little coke . . . slept around some, but God finally brought me to my senses."

Because I hadn't done *any* of those things. I was just one of those "good kids" that the teachers loved.

(Well, I *did* have to stand out in the hall once in third grade for talking. . . .)

But as I entered college I began to realize the rewards of living the "straight life." I wasn't haunted by memories I was trying to forget. I

93

had no regrets in my language, my dating life, or my friendships. I could actually feel *proud* of my past.

God rewards those who place him first and keep him first. Now before you think I'm bragging, I have to let you know that I couldn't live a straight life in my own strength. Only through the power of the Holy Spirit (God living inside me) was I able as a teen to say no to the things he didn't want me mixed up in.

I now realize that I have a unique and wonderful testimony. Even though I've never messed around sexually, cussed, tasted alcohol, or smoked, I remember what I was *before* Jesus became Lord of my life . . . and I can see what he's still helping me become *after* I gave him complete control.

I used to be an extremely self-centered person. God is teaching me to focus more on others rather than myself. I used to feel like I lived in a

rut—same old thing, same old existence. When Jesus came into my heart, he filled me with an enthusiasm for life. He gave me a definite reason and purpose for life. Now every single day holds fresh meaning for me!

I'm excited to walk hand-in-hand with the Creator of the Universe! He knows my name! He's on *my* side. He knows me inside and out—better than anyone else in the whole world. (Yep, he knows that a lot of times I'm a twirp . . . but he continues to stick with me . . . even promised he'd never leave!)

And guess what? Not only does he *know* me better than anyone else, he *loves* me *more* than anyone else does, too! I get pretty jazzed about that.

So it doesn't matter that, like Boring Barry, I've never done many of the things others use in their testimonies. The important thing is

Reflecting . . .

1 Why is it OK to not have a "dramatic" testimony?

2 What are the advantages

that God forgave *me* of *my* sin (because we're *all* born with it . . . and is getting drunk really any worse than gossiping? Not to God!), and through his power he is helping me to live a godly life.

Sometimes I get tired of hearing about all the bad. I like hearing from someone who can say, "I haven't done any of that. And it's not because I'm strong or cool or have my act together. It's because God gives me the strength to withstand."

And guess what?

He'll give *you* that strength, too!

(Now that you realize *everyone* has a testimony, keep reading to find out how you can share God's love without being a geek. But if you're tired of sitting, stand up and put your shoes on the wrong feet, swallow some Gatorade, and try to talk Mom into ordering a pizza tonight . . . *then* turn the page, OK?)

How to Shout without Screaming

At the sound of the bell, I (Susie) collected yesterday's homework assignment—then grabbed the chalkboard railing for protection—as thirty-two high-school juniors raced out of my classroom and down the hall.

I thought I'd seen it all: Mike peeling his scabs when he was supposed to be taking notes; Jason stapling his thumb to the desk; and even Mary Beth trying to sneak a pepperoni-with-extra-pepperoni thin-crust pizza into class, insisting it was "doctor's orders" for her unique diet. Shawn, however, took me by surprise.

As he pushed his way through the crowded hallway, I noticed both his hands were full. One held the hand of brown-haired, hazel-eyed Kari; the other balanced his stack of books. It was the stack of books that intrigued me.

On the very bottom I noticed *French II* with scrunched papers slipping out the side. On top of the French book, I saw his biology text, and I smiled, remembering the funeral he'd given his frog before Mrs. Hike made him dissect it. On top of

the biology book, I noticed his speech text and was glad he was prepared for *my* class. On top of his speech book, I noticed a black book with gold lettering on the cover.

In overhearing some of his hallway conversation with other classmates (and by reading the journal he had to keep as a class assignment), I found out that he'd recently committed his life to Christ. According to his journal entry, Shawn wanted to make a godly impact on the kids in his world. I had to admit, bringing his Bible to school would certainly make an impact!

A Change Occurred

Shawn was well liked and respected at school. Not only was he on the football team, but he was also class president. I was excited about his potential testimony and watched him carefully.

When he finished an assignment early, he pulled out his Bible and read. He copied Scripture verses on notebook paper and tried to memorize them weekly. He still laughed, and he still had the respect of his classmates, but it was obvious a change had occurred in his life.

When others bragged about what they did over the weekend—how much beer they could hold or told about their new boyfriend/girlfriend—Shawn listened.

When Dave laughed about wrecking his dad's "beemer" because he was too stoned to see straight and Tami told about not even knowing her date's last name, Shawn listened.

And finally when the others asked him what *he* did over the weekend, he responded, "I went to church."

"Church! You're kidding."

"Yeah, I went to church."

"But what'd you do for *fun?*"

Shawn's familiar smile stretched across his face as he continued. "I go to church because I *want* to. I've made some changes in my life, and I want to make sure I stay on the right track."

While the others nailed him for being so straight, Shawn stood his ground. Never losing his smile, he firmly, yet politely, told how he couldn't do the things they did. When they drilled him, he responded. When they questioned, he answered. When they ridiculed, he smiled and continued to share. And guess what? He never lost the respect of his classmates.

In Love with Him

Amy, meanwhile, was across the hall talking excitedly about Friday night's game. She was a cheerleader. I noticed Katie apart from the group. She pretended to get something out of her locker, but I knew she longed for acceptance. It wasn't long before Amy made an effort to include her in the conversation.

"Katie, I didn't see you at the game Friday night. Were you there?"

"No, I . . . I didn't have a ride," she stammered nervously.

"I usually ride with my brother. If you want to go, we'd be glad to pick you up next Friday."

Katie was a loner. I was impressed that Amy was willing to go out of her way for her. But that was Amy. She seemed to glow with confidence and enthusiasm. More than once, I'd seen her share her joy with a lonely face or a new student.

Amy literally wore her Christianity through her happiness. But it wasn't a phony happiness, it was *real*. She'd gone through some deep waters and had her own share of problems. But she was so in love with Christ that the satisfaction from a deep walk with him seemed to spill out onto her relationships with classmates.

Speaking Volumes

The bell rang and jarred my attention toward my own classroom. I glanced at the roll and checked off the attendance. Amid the scuffling of feet and beginning of class laughter, I heard Joey ask Michelle for

last night's assignment. (It wasn't often that anyone tried to cheat off Michelle, because her answers were usually wrong, but once in a while a desperate victim would forget.)

"Did you finish that study sheet for class today?" quizzed Joey.

"Yeah."

"Good. Lemme see it."

"Aw, Joey, get your own answers."

"C'mon, Michelle! She's gonna collect them any minute. Let me have your sheet!"

Michelle stood her ground. "No, Joey. I don't cheat. I'll be glad to help you next time if you don't understand the assignment, but I can't let you have my study sheet."

I collected the papers before Joey had a chance to beg anyone else for help, and I winked at Michelle as I passed her desk.

Michelle wasn't the most popular girl in school, or even in my class, but she had her own circle of friends, and people respected her for what she believed.

Michelle never ran for a class office, never tried out for the school drama production, and was never nominated for homecoming queen, but she always had a smile and a ready supply of laughter for those around her.

She failed most of her tests, was tardy sometimes, and talked when she should have been listening. Still . . . there was something about her.

In her own special way, she exhibited a strong relationship with Christ that was obvious to the other students. In today's blackboard jungle, where it seems like "everybody does it," the fact that Michelle didn't party, didn't cheat, and didn't lie spoke volumes to hundreds of other students who did.

Making an Imprint

As I walked toward my car, Coach Hendren's instructions interrupted my thoughts. "Liebman, Riley, Adams! You guys are getting lazy. You want to be on second string the rest of your life? Everyone take six laps and hit the showers."

Andy threw the football down and began running. I watched from the parking lot, trying to imagine what he was thinking: *Maybe if I increase my weight lifts and get in an extra mile, I can make first string by the third or fourth game.*

As he passed the edge of the chain link fence by my car, I coughed through the scattered dirt his cleats left and focused on the imprint his shoes left on the ground.

Andy, too, made an imprint. Not a bold one like his brother Pete, who was first-string quarterback and president of the student body, but a definite mark nonetheless.

Living in the shadow of his older

brother didn't seem to bother him. Andy often bragged on Pete and joked about what a terrific brother he was, even though he'd forgotten to clean out the dirty sock bag last week.

Both Pete and Andy were Christians and well respected by the student body. Even though Pete was outspoken and funny and had a magnetic personality, he depended on the quiet strength of his younger brother.

Andy had a positive attitude that was almost contagious. And within that positive outlook, strength and sensitivity were found.

Andy certainly wasn't the life of the party like his brother Pete, but he was friendly. I smiled, remembering the Mr. Friendly Award he received last year. While Pete made a bold impact on others through his dynamic personality, Andy made an impact through simply being friendly. They were both genuine.

Reflect God Himself

As I backed out of the school parking lot, I reflected on the excitement of serving a God who uses a variety of individual personalities to make an impact for him.

It was refreshing to be reminded that I didn't have to be preachy or freaky to communicate my faith.

To find out more about Andy and Pete—alias, the apostles Andrew and Peter—read Matthew, Mark, Luke, or John. To discover more about Shawn, Amy, or Michelle, watch those around you—or even look at yourself.

It doesn't matter which personality category you fall into. What *does* matter is that your life-style reflects God himself. Your actions, your willingness to befriend an uncool student, and your values will SHOUT volumes to lost friends who need Christ's direction.

―――――――――Reflecting . . .―――――――

1 Think about your school. Does anyone you know resemble Shawn, Amy, Michelle, Andy, or Pete?

2 What do people think of straight-laced kids?

3 Can you think of three things *you* can do to "shout" without screaming?

What to Say... What Not to Say

OK. OK. OK. Enough *reading* about sharing your faith. Let's practice.

Situation:

You and your friend John tried out for the basketball team. You both got cut. John's pretty bummed. You are too, naturally, but *you* have an inner strength that John doesn't have. He says, "How can you keep your cool when you've just been cut?"

Bad response: "I never wanted to play for our lousy team anyway. They're all a bunch of wimps. I'll probably join a city league. Want to come with me to get some info?"

Good response: "Actually I'm pretty bummed, too. But John, even though making the team was really important to me, it's not everything.

I have something else in my life that's even *more* important." (Way to go! Now you're wide open. Let *him* pursue the conversation, though. If he doesn't, be happy knowing you planted a seed. Trust God to open another door at another time.)

WHERE'D YOU GET THE DORKO HAIRDO?

103

Situation:

Mindy is really worried about her English grade. She's on the verge of failing, and her parents have told her if she doesn't pass she'll be grounded for two months. She says, "You gotta help me cheat! It's my only chance of passing this stupid class and having a normal social life."

Bad response: "Sure, Mindy. You can cheat off me anytime!"

Good response: "I don't feel right about cheating, but I'll be glad to help you study. Maybe that seems weird to you, 'cause I know everyone cheats, but, well . . . I'm a Christian, and cheating is something I believe God doesn't want me involved in." (Good comeback. You've given her absolutely no hope for cheating off you, while at the same time partly explaining why you don't cheat. If she's curious, she'll follow up with a *why.* If not, at least you've let your values be known.)

Bad response: "The teacher is already offering extra help before and after school. If you weren't so stupid, maybe you'd grab a clue and catch on!"

Good response: "Sorry, Mindy. I don't cheat. I'm also not real good at English and am struggling myself. But I'll help you find someone who *does* know what they're doing. I could use the help too. Meanwhile . . . I'll be praying for you, OK?"

(Great. You turned down her cheating request, but you offered to pray for her. This keeps her from feeling as though you've let her down. She'll sense your sincerity.)

Situation:

Rod has been saying unkind things about you at school and making fun of your beliefs. Your feelings have been deeply hurt. You're guessing it all started when you ran against him for student council and won. He says, "Going to homecoming Friday night? Or does your church have revival? You probably don't believe in having fun, anyway!"

Bad response: "Rod, you're a real geekburger, you know it? Still jealous because I beat you in the elections?"

Good response: "I *love* to have fun, Rod . . . but not at other people's expense. Yeah, I'll be going to homecoming. Oh, and Rod, our church revival is *next* week. How 'bout if I swing by and pick you up? I'll even spring for a Coke afterwards . . . that is, if you think you can stand being around a religious freak for an entire evening." (Good job. By poking fun at yourself you've let him know that there are more important issues in life than his bugging you. It's my guess he won't bother you much longer, and he'll also be thinking about what makes you so different.)

Situation:

It's Friday night, and several of your friends have invited you to go to an R-rated movie. Besides needing to obey your parents' rules about not attending, you know this particular movie will mess you up spiritually. It has some sex scenes that will linger in your mind a lot longer than the aftertaste of last night's fish Mom made you eat. You don't want to sound like a prude, but you *do* want to take a stand. They say, "It starts at eight o'clock. You backed out on us last time, so you *gotta* come this time. Let's go!"

Bad response: "I really don't have the money. You guys go ahead. But ask me again next time, OK?"

Good response: "I know that movie has some funny lines in it, but I also know it's got some stuff that's gonna be hard for me to forget. God and I are working overtime to get my thoughts cleaned up, and that's the last thing I need. Why don't you come over *here?* We can rent a couple of videos, and I'll talk Mom into making her special Mississippi mud cake. And if you're here by seven, you can have it straight from the oven—hot and oozing with chocolate." (Yeah! You haven't put them down for wanting to go, you've explained why you *don't* want to go, and you've given them a better option for the evening. Chances are, if they accept your invitation, you'll have another opportunity before the night's over to share a little more about your relationship with Christ.)

Reflecting . . .

1 List a couple of other common situations. What would be a bad/good response?

2 How can you learn to change your bad responses to good ones?

Every Day for a Whole Year!

In ninth grade, a new girl enrolled in our school. Her name was Debbie Volk. She was in my fourth-, fifth-, and sixth-period classes. And since we were seated in alphabetical order in those classes—and since *her* last name started with a *V* and mine with an *S*—we sat right across the aisle from each other every day for a year.

Debbie had a magnetic personality. She smiled a lot, laughed easily, and was just a lot of fun to hang out with. People—including me—were drawn to her.

Well, I was certainly enjoying being her friend and couldn't help but think how great she'd fit in with our youth group. I wasn't sure if she was a Christian, but I really wanted her to be exposed to the power God had to offer. Besides that, I knew she'd be a big hit with my other friends at

church. I wanted her to be a part of it all!

So I invited her to church. She got real excited and said she'd love to come but she'd have to check with her parents first. The next day she gave me the bad news. "They said

PAT!
PAT!
PAT!

SEEDS

no, Susie. They won't let me go to your church."

So I waited a couple of days and invited her to a Sunday school contest our youth group was having. "Deb, you just gotta come! I want you on my team, and who knows? Maybe I'll win and I'll split the prize with you. First place is a chauffeured limo for a whole day. Just think . . . we could ride to school in style!"

She was dying to come. Said she'd run it by her folks. But the next day was just as big a letdown as before. "They said, no, Susie. They don't want me attending church."

I waited a few days and tried again. "Deb, we're having revival at church. And the speaker is really fun and exciting and Friday night is youth night and we've all got reserved seats down front and afterward we're having this huge pizza party and you just gotta come, Deb! The kids in our group would go crazy over you!"

She was jazzed. Pizza, special seats down front. Sounded good. But the next day brought the same bad news. "They said no, Susie. They won't let me go to church."

I waited a few more days, then hit her again. "Deb, this Sunday night at church we're showing this really cool film. It's awesome, Deb! And afterward our youth group is

having the world's largest banana split. So you *gotta* come, Deb! The film's gonna be good . . . and all the ice cream you can eat. You just can't miss it, Deb."

Yeah. It *did* sound good. She really wanted to come. So she promised to *beg* her parents this time. But . . . you guessed it. The next day brought the same ol' answer. "They said no, Susie. I can't go to church with you."

OK. So I changed my strategy. Our youth minister had just started an early morning devotional/fun time in our school cafeteria (yep, in a public school—shows ya the power of prayer, huh?) once a week every Tuesday morning for fifteen minutes before school began.

I was pumped. "Deb, this isn't really church. And it's not even *in* the church! And our youth minister comes out every week, and we get free donuts and juice. And he brings his guitar, and we sing crazy songs. And a whole bunch of people are coming—we had a hundred and fifty last week! And Deb, I want you to be a part of it! And I want you to meet Doug, our youth minister. So can you come? 'Cause it's not really *church* church. It's just *us* in the school cafeteria."

There was hope in her eyes. "Well, yeah, maybe so. I mean . . . you're right, it's not really *church*

church. Maybe they *will* let me come!"

I prayed hard that Deb would be allowed to come. But the next day when she arrived at school, I could see the answer written all over her face. "They said no, Susie. Since it's sponsored by a church they kind of consider it church. So, I'm really sorry, but I can't go."

Almost every day for a year I invited Debbie Volk to *something*. Whether it was a missionary service or a burger bash, I kept letting her know I really wanted her to be a part of our youth group.

And almost every day for a year, Debbie Volk said no.

After ninth grade, we left junior high and entered high school. Even though we attended the same school, it was so large we didn't ever see each other. We had no classes together, and I don't think we even passed each other in the halls. For the next three years I lost contact with Debbie.

After high-school graduation I enrolled in a private Christian college in town. I'll never forget the day I moved into the dorm. I walked down the hall with loaded arms and suddenly stopped in front of room 412. My eyes bugged out, and I almost dropped my sheets, pillows, and towels.

Debbie Volk was unpacking boxes and filling drawers in room

412. "Debbie! What're you doing here? You couldn't even come to my *church*. What're you doing at my *college?*"

She laughed, and her eyes twinkled with enthusiasm. "A couple of years ago a Christian couple moved next door to our family. They formed a friendship with my parents and eventually led them to the Lord. We've been going to church for a year and a half now! I'm here at our church college enrolled for school." Then she laughed again. "Susie, I'm gonna be here for the next four years!"

Wow. Does God answer prayer, or what?

After college graduation Debbie married a youth minister. I saw them a few years ago at a youth ministry conference. She pulled me aside and said, "Susie, thanks for inviting me to church almost every day for a whole year."

"Why?" I laughed. "You never came."

"Yeah, but you'll never know how much I *wanted* to. You were so excited about God and your youth group and everything that was going on in your church. *I* wanted what *you* had." Then Deb got quiet. After a few seconds, she continued.

"I gotta tell you that you really planted the seed. I guess it was God's will for someone else to come along and water it and make it grow. But Susie, *you* planted the seed. Thanks."

Wow. A seed-planter. I like that. And I like to think that every time *you* invite someone to church or a youth group function, *you're* planting a seed also. Don't get discouraged when you're turned down (even if it's almost every day for a whole year) . . . you never know what kind of seed you're planting.

God will do the rest. It's *his* re-sponsibility to water, to spark growth, to produce fruit. It's *our* job to be seed-planters. A quiet testimony. That's all it took. Just a little enthusiasm about my own walk with Christ and what he was doing personally in my life. Quiet testimonies. Consistency. Excitement about the fact that *you* know the Creator of the Universe! Can there be *anything* more powerful for reaching your friends?

Reflecting . . .

1 What are some events at your church that you feel comfortable inviting your friends to?

2 Want to be a seed-planter? Think of two people you could invite to something at your church this month.

CHAPTER 25

If at First You Don't Succeed...

All of us who have ever tried to share our faith have one thing in common: failure. Or so we think, anyway.

- We build a friendship with someone, but they have no interest in God, Jesus, or the Bible.
- We spend so much time with a buddy that they're able to see us at our worst—and we haven't disappointed them.
- They've asked questions we couldn't answer, like: Who was Cain's wife? Where is the ark? How could human men write a perfect Bible? Did Adam have a belly button? Can God make a rock he can't lift?
- We have the desire to see a friend come to know Christ, but we haven't prayed for them

or prayed for opportunities to explain what we believe.

- Or maybe someone was ready to trust Christ and we didn't know how to lead them in the right direction. In fact, we could only think of one verse—

John 3:16—that even talked about God's plan.

What do we do when we feel we've done something that has delayed or—in our minds—*prevented* someone from becoming a Christian?

In chapter 38 we're going to learn what to do when we make a mistake, but until we get there, here's the short version: recognize it, admit it, learn from it, and forget it.

Persevering through mistakes or unconscious blunders is how we grow. God is well aware that we're not the most perfect representatives. In fact, he's aware that sometimes we're the *least* perfect! Yet he knows we need to learn to die to ourselves and start living for others. That's when the abundant life (John 10:10) really begins to kick in.

The Perfect Setup

One day, Jesus and his disciples rowed their boat across the Sea of Galilee to Boston. (OK . . . so Boston wasn't invented yet. It was really the region of the Gerasenes. But we can pretend it was Boston, right?) As soon as he got out of the boat, here's what happened:

A man with an evil spirit came from the tombs to meet him. This man lived in the tombs, and no one could bind him any more, not even

with a chain. For he had often been chained hand and foot, but he tore the chains apart and broke the irons on his feet. No one was strong enough to subdue him. Night and day among the tombs and in the hills he would cry out and cut himself with stones. (Mark 5:2-5)

Not someone you'd want to share a locker with, huh? Or even a lunch table, for that matter! But Jesus cares enough to find out more. Like the fact that this guy is possessed by thousands of demons. The demons begged Jesus to leave them alone, but he sent them into a herd of pigs who rumbled off a cliff into the sea.

The pig herders raced into town, and everyone came out to the place where it happened.

When they came to Jesus, they saw the man who had been possessed by the legion of demons, sitting there, dressed and in his right mind; and they were afraid. (Mark 5:15)

Here's a guy who was just *slightly* worse than your average high-school football player, but was miraculously delivered from satanic bondage by Jesus. How many months do you think it would take before his conversation skills, table manners, and personal hygiene were up to speed? You guessed it . . . lots! But Jesus gave *him* the same type of challenge he gives *us:* "Go home to your family and tell them how much the Lord has done for you, and how he has had mercy on you" (5:19).

Our ex-demon-possessed friend originally wanted to hang out with Jesus and his buddies for a while. After all, he'd never been taught how to explain to someone the booklet *Your Most Important Relationship.* He didn't even know how to find Philippians in the New Testament (since there wasn't one yet, I guess that would have been tough to do). And he didn't have a hot youth group to invite his friends to. So what did he do?

The man went away and began to tell in the Decapolis how much Jesus had done for him. And all the people were amazed. (5:20)

Instead of thinking he didn't know anything, he headed out to Decapolis (a region of ten cities around the Sea of Galilee) and told everyone what Jesus had done for him. I wonder if he made any mistakes. I wonder if he got tongue-tied trying to explain how God had changed him. I wonder if he faced any rejection. . . .

No need to really wonder. The answer to all three is most likely yes!

I wonder if Jesus knew that by ▼

sending him out "untrained" he would make mistakes, not know what to say, and occasionally get rejected.

Jesus knew *exactly* what would happen. (He knows everything.)

He knows the setbacks you'll face, too.

Are You Looking for a Sign?

Satan would have us think that minor setbacks are a sign from God that we aren't "gifted." Or we don't have "God's blessing." Or that we should "leave it to professionals."

Please memorize this fact: **Inexperience, rejection, apathy by others, and setbacks ARE NOT a sign for you to give up.** In reality, they're more likely a sign that Satan is aware of your efforts and is trying to discourage you from developing a lifetime habit of reaching others for the Savior. He'll wave any shred of resistance in your face and try to convince you to settle for church activities that don't involve risk. He tried that strategy on the apostle Paul. Remember? He was the guy who once tried to kill Christians. Here are a few "minor setbacks" he faced while obeying the call to tell the world about what Christ had done for him:

I have worked much harder, been in prison more frequently, been flogged more severely, and been exposed to death again and again. Five times I received from the Jews the forty lashes minus one. Three times I was beaten with rods, once I was stoned, three times I was shipwrecked, I spent a night and a day in the open sea, I have been constantly on the move. I have been in danger from rivers, in danger from bandits, in danger from my own countrymen, in danger from Gentiles; in danger in the city, in danger in the country, in danger at sea; and in danger from false brothers. I have labored and toiled and have often gone without sleep; I have known hunger and thirst and have often gone without food; I have been cold and naked. (2 Corinthians 11:23-27)

WHEW!!!

True, all this didn't occur at Tarsus High when Paul was a teenager. It happened within the next thirty years after he'd found Christ. He

had the wisdom to see through Satan's schemes and not let outward circumstances change his inner motivation to share his faith. No, he wasn't Super-Christian. I'm sure there were times he really felt discouraged—times when he asked himself if it was all worth it. But he persevered because he knew the stakes were high: A relationship with Christ on this earth and eternity in heaven instead of hell was just too much to keep to himself.

Be assured, God knows what you can handle as you seek to persevere, too. Maybe that's why you haven't been shipwrecked lately. But he also knows that pressing on—in spite of the setbacks you'll face—will ultimately give you the results you want.

Let us not become weary in doing good, for at the proper time we will reap a harvest if we do not give up. (Galatians 6:9)

Reflecting . . .

1 What trials or mistakes have you faced trying to share your faith?

2 Have they discouraged you to the point of wanting to give up?

Developing Your Story

WOW! You're personal friends with the Creator of the Universe! Naturally, you want to share your faith with those around you, but how? You need a tool. Some equipment. You need a *testimony*. (And before you start thinking, *I've never done drugs, I don't have a testimony!* flip back to page 93. Remember, Susie didn't either, but she still has a testimony—and so do you!)

(And before *you* start thinking, *I've done too much—I'm not sure I'm really worthy of sharing my testimony,* remember that God has the power to make BEAUTIFUL things happen out of devastating situations.)

Everyone has a testimony. The issue right now is putting it together so you can share it with others. Let's work it like a puzzle.

Cool. I like puzzles.

Good. This will be the most important puzzle you'll ever put together in your whole life.

Wow.

Yeah. *Double* wow. Stick with me.

OK.

You don't want your testimony to be a thirty-minute sermon. Strive to keep it around three minutes so your friend won't daydream himself into the ozone layer while you're droning on and on.

And try to be excited! After all, you're sharing the most important thing in your life! So be interesting. Use your past experiences. Listeners relate better to personal stories. This will arouse interest.

Share some Scripture. This is important so you can back up what you're saying.

Uh oh. Trouble spot. I don't know a whole lot of Scripture.

It's OK. I'll give you some verses. But start reading your Bible more, and try to memorize some key verses, OK?

Gotcha.

One more thing. When you get ready to give your testimony to someone, strive to be sensitive with your language.

Whattaya mean?

Well, instead of saying, "Can I tell you about something exciting in my life?" try saying, "Can I share something exciting in my life?" There's a diff between *telling* and *sharing*.

Know whatcha mean. "Telling" makes me think of someone pointing their finger at me and coming down hard.

You got it.

But "sharing" . . . well, that sounds more friendly.

Exactly. And that's what you want—a friendly situation. No one likes to feel stressed or trapped into listening to something.

Yeah.

Even though there are only three pieces to this puzzle, each piece is majorly important.

First Piece: Your Life BEFORE You Met Christ

What was your life-style like? What did you think? Include attitude and habits. Examples: "I was selfish. I thought about using others to get ahead. I was only interested in what I could get out of life. I partied a lot, always searching for something better . . . anything that would make me feel good for the moment was an option."

Second Piece: How You Came to Know Christ

Be specific with this. Don't say something like, "Then I met Christ, and everything changed for the better." *How* did you meet him? Share where and when, too.

(Some people honestly can't remember a *specific* time when they became a Christian. That's OK. Don't start thinking you'll be banned from heaven just because you can't come up with a certain date. *No one* is *just born* a Christian. We *all* have to make a decision to follow Christ and actually ask him to forgive our sins and take control of our lives. You may remember a general time in your life rather than a specific day and year when this happened. Share that.)

You also want to emphasize that your relationship with Christ is a *free gift*. Make sure your friend understands that he can't earn it. You may want to create an illustration of giving a present to him. It's not really his until he accepts it.

Examples of how one could come to know Christ: "I was at a Christian concert, and the singer challenged us to let God take control of our lives. I knew *I* was sure tired of being in charge and going nowhere. So, when he asked us to stand up if we wanted to make that decision, I stood. It was then that I prayed and accepted God's gift of forgiveness."

Or . . .

"Our youth group had a winter retreat. I was really searching for some answers. Besides feeling lonely, I just lacked a purpose for living. Life didn't make much sense to me. On Saturday night our youth leader said he was going to pray out loud, and if any of us wanted to accept Christ as our Savior, we could repeat the prayer silently. So ▼

I did. That's how I met Christ. Now he lives inside me and is changing my life for the better!"

Third Piece: Your Life AFTER You Met Christ

Share the *specific* changes that have happened as a result of making Jesus Lord of your life. Share what Christ means to you now. Talk about the excitement you experience from your relationship with him.

Be careful to avoid giving the impression that your life is now free from problems, because realistically, *everyone* will continue to face hardship. Share the difference: Now you have someone to face the hard times *with* you and provide the wisdom and strength to handle them.

Examples of specific changes: "Now I have a reason to live. Everything is in perspective. He's given me a genuine concern for other people. I really *want* to help others. I'm not always thinking about myself—I'm learning how to meet the needs of those around me."

"Every day is a *new* day. It blows my mind that he loves me even though he knows I'm still a jerk a lot of times. Life is kind of like an adventure now. I mean, I'm walking hand-in-hand with the Master of the Universe!"

Scripture

The following Scripture passages provide more information on how you became a Christian. You might want to use some of these in your testimony; if not, keep them handy to answer any questions your friend might have. These are also great verses to memorize!

John 3:16: For God so loved the world that he gave his one and only Son, that whoever believes in him shall not perish but have eternal life.

Romans 3:23: For all have sinned and fall short of the glory of God.

Romans 5:8: But God demonstrates his own love for us in this: While we were still sinners, Christ died for us.

John 1:12: Yet to all who received him, to those who believed in his name, he gave the right to become children of God.

OK, *your* turn. Using the space below, put the pieces to your own testimony together. Then, read it out loud, and time yourself to see if it's too long or too short. When you've honed it to approximately three minutes, ask your parents or youth minister or Christian friend if you can practice it on them.

118

MY PERSONAL TESTIMONY
1. My life before I met Christ

_____

_____

_____

_____

_____

_____

_____

_____

_____

_____

_____

_____

_____

_____

_____

_____

_____

_____

_____

_____

2. How I came to know Christ

_____

_____

_____

_____

_____

_____

_____

_____

_____

_____

_____

_____

_____

_____

_____

_____

_____

3. My life after I met Christ

_____

_____

_____

_____

_____

_____

_____

_____

_____

_____

_____

_____

_____

_____

_____

_____

_____

119

Giving Your Personal Testimony

Now that you have your own personal testimony, let's chat for a sec about how you present it.

Whattaya mean? I just GIVE it, right?

Well, yeah . . . but there are some other things worth mentioning that'll help you feel good about yourself when sharing it.

I WILL be kinda nervous.

And that's OK. You're normal.

Yeah, you already told me that in chapter 3, remember?

OK. OK. But sometimes it's good to be reminded. Anyway, you wanna feel CONFIDENT when sharing Christ, so let's chat about what can help.

You mean stuff like not having a piece of broccoli stuck between my teeth?

Exactly. Here are some confidence boosters.

The Way You Look

You may be the only picture of Jesus your friend has ever seen. So, naturally, you want to look your best. And besides, when you *look* good, you *feel* good. Result? Confidence.

This is simple stuff, really. Basics

121

like making sure your hair isn't shifting out to another galaxy, having good breath (I'm serious! This can be a real turnoff!), and just looking like you're well put together.

Exception: You're in the locker room. The time is right. The friend you've been praying for suddenly seems interested in knowing more about Christ. You're in his world—go ahead and share your testimony. He'll relate.

DON'T jump up, run home and change clothes, come back, and give your testimony. That's silly. Use common sense, mon.

The Way You Think

Ask God to help you zero in on little clues your friends might be dropping that hint of their interest in knowing more about your relationship. Learn to be a quick thinker. Be alert! Listen for golden opportuni-

ties in class, the hallways, your school cafeteria, the practice field. Keep your spiritual eyes and ears open!

The Way You Talk

We've already shared a little about certain things to say/not to say . . . but watch your general conversation as well. Don't tell questionable jokes just to get a laugh. It's natural to want to be included by your non-Christian friends so you can eventually share Christ with them . . . but if you're being included at the expense of being *like* them instead of being *different,* your testimony will never be heard.

Strive to maintain a positive attitude. Sometimes this is re-e-e-ally hard in the blackboard jungle—especially when Mrs. Moffett never lets up on homework—but your lifestyle and attitude will speak much

Reflecting . . .

1 Do you need to make any changes in your outward appearance or inward attitude as you start sharing your faith?

2 What else is important to remember when sharing your faith?

louder than your words. If you're confident about your actions, you'll be confident in giving your testimony.

The Way You Time It

Only God can provide the perfect timing, that golden opportunity, the exact right moment to share. If you try to force it or make it happen in ● your own power, you won't feel the confidence you need to be effective.

The Holy Spirit (God's personality and power living inside you) will guide and direct. Learn to depend on *him* to help you discern the right time to share your testimony. When the timing is *God's timing,* you'll be much more confident in sharing him with others.

Practice Makes Perfect

OK, now that you've *read* about sharing your faith and read about *practicing* sharing your faith, it's time to rehearse. Let's do some role playing, OK? (I can't help it, I'm an ex–high-school drama teacher!)

Grab a few friends from youth group, and take turns responding to the following situations. I'll get you started with a few lines in each scenario. After that, you're on your own!

Situation 1

Doug's dad has been in a car wreck. You're not *super* close to Doug, but he *is* in your third-period history class. You sit across the aisle from each other and are casual friends. Doug's not a Christian and is not from a Christian family.

Doug: Wow. I really bombed this ▼

test. Guess my mind's been on Dad. I'm really worried about him.

You: I'm sorry, Doug. How bad is he?

Doug: He's not gonna die or anything. He just broke a leg and two ribs. But it's weird seeing him

TAKE 97!

SCENE II

125

all helpless in the hospital, you know?

You: Yeah. Hospitals give me the willies.

Doug: But, you know, hanging around during visiting hours and peeking into some of the other rooms and stuff has really made me think.

You: About what?

Doug: Life. Death. Where you go after you die.

You:

Situation 2

Missy and Brad just broke up after going together for eleven months. She's totally devastated.

Missy: I can't believe it's over.

You: Missy, I'm really sorry. I know you're hurting big-time, and I also want you to know I'm here for you.

Missy: You don't understand. How could he do this to me? I mean, he said he loved me!

You: Missy, look . . . you're terrific. It doesn't matter what one guy thinks or does.

Missy: It *does* matter! How can I ever be happy again?

You:

Situation 3

Jason's family just moved to your city. He's not a Christian, but he *does* have a close-knit family and

good values—and he's a lot of fun to be around. You're becoming friends. You want to invite him to church and eventually lead him to Christ. He seems interested.

Jason: So whattaya doin' this Friday night?

You: Goin' to a pizza party.

Jason: Really? Sounds like fun.

You: It's with our youth group from church.

Jason: Are they fun people?

You: Yep. But they'd be *more* fun if they knew you!

Jason: I don't know . . . I'm not really "into" church.

You: Got better plans?

Jason: No . . . and I *do* like pizza.

You: I'll pick you up at five-thirty.

Jason: Why are you so involved in church, anyway?

You:

Situation 4

You've been friends with Jill for a long time. She's come to church with you often but has never made a decision to follow Christ. Recently, it seems like nothing has gone her way. You sense that she's finally close to accepting Christ as her Savior.

Jill: Can't believe the Wilsons are moving. They were my best baby-sitting income. Now I'll never have money to do anything!

You: Ah, come on, Jill. You'll find other baby-sitting jobs.

Jill: I don't think so. Dad grounded me from all means of making money until I bring up my math grade. That could take forever!

You (*chuckling*): Yeah, you're right, it could. Your math grades are pretty low.

Jill: So how come you've always got it so together?

You: Me? Together? I may be doing OK in math, but history? Well, that's another story.

Jill: Yeah, but you know what I mean. No matter how much rotten stuff gets tossed your way, you just keep on going.

You: It's my relationship with God, Jill. You know that. We've talked about this before.

Jill: Yeah, I know we've *talked* about it . . . but lately I've really been *thinking* about it.

You: Yeah?

Jill: Yeah. I'm tired of feeling like my life's going nowhere fast. I want what you have.

You:

Good job! It was even kind of fun, wasn't it? Now trust the Lord to continue helping you develop skills for sharing your faith. Ask him to bring you some exciting opportunities this week.

Reflecting . . .

1 Now that you're on a roll, create two more role-play situations and get some friends to help you act them out.

Surefire Starters for Reaching Out

Dear Susie:

My parents don't want me hanging around with the wrong crowd, but doesn't Jesus want us to be friends with people who don't know him? How can I reach out to the "bad" kids if I don't hang out with them?

ST. LOUIS, MISSOURI

I appreciate your concern for those who don't know Christ. I think you and your parents are *both* right. Yes, Jesus wants us to reach out to those who don't know him . . . but there's a big diff between *reaching out* and *forming intimate relationships.*

You can purchase soft drinks in a bar, but why go into the bar just to get a Coke? That's placing yourself in an unnecessary environment of temptation. Should you attend ▼

the big party Friday night just so you can make a stand? (Read what Shane did in "Being Different Makes a Difference!" on page 137.)

Yes, Jesus hung out with sinners . . . but they weren't sinners for very long. They couldn't help but notice

129

he was different, and they wanted what he had to offer.

I think your parents are probably concerned that if you become really tight with the wrong crowd, it could influence your actions and decisions. Know what? They're right! We can't *help* but be affected by those we hang around with. *They* either influence you, or *you* influence them.

So, how do you be "in" the world but not "of" the world?

How 'bout following these sure-fire starters?

Make Contact

You're partly right. If we're going to impact others for Christ, we'll have to *make contact*. A silent witness is powerful, but at some point we're going to have to say or do something. God doesn't want you to be a wallflower and simply withdraw from non-Christians. In fact, he wants just the opposite:

> *For the Holy Spirit, God's gift, does not want you to be afraid of people, but to be wise and strong, and to love them and enjoy being with them. If you will stir up this inner power, you will never be afraid to tell others about our Lord. (2 Timothy 1:7-8, TLB)*

So how can you reach out and make contact? *By being friendly.* Keep a smile on your face. Laugh a lot. Non-Christians don't have the joy *you* have from a close relationship with the Lord. Believe it or not, they'll be attracted to your life-style that reflects *fun*.

Your school has tons of "built-in" ways of making contact: clubs, lunchtime, classes, sports, and various other activities. Take advantage of these (without becoming overloaded, of course), and use the opportunities to make contact.

Find Common Ground

In Luke 5:7-8 you'll notice that Jesus dealt with what people were interested in. If the non-Christian guys in your second-period class are really "into" championship wrestling, you probably won't get very far trying to talk with them about painting. There's no common ground. Build a bridge and deal with *their* interests.

Always? No. There will be exceptions. For example, if the kids at your cafeteria table are interested in slamming the new girl and are saying dirty things about her, it wouldn't be a good idea for you to jump in and join them just to find that common ground. Use your head! You wanna be Jesus to them, remember?

How can you find common ground? *Ask questions* and *listen.* You'll be surprised how much you'll learn if you really try. People **love** to talk about what concerns them. Many Christians make the mistake of talking too much. You'll find out a ton of information by simply giving others a chance to express themselves.

Don't Put Others Down

Your non-Christian classmates don't need you to be a preacher. Chances are, they've had their fill of TV preachers and other adults who try to "preach" their convictions at them. What they need is to see a *positive difference* in your life!

Joey comes to first period with bloodshot eyes from his wild weekend. Mr. Buchanan gives a written assignment to the class that's due at the end of the hour. Joey has barely managed to get *himself* to class. He couldn't even think about *supplies* like a pen or a notebook. How will you respond?

A. "Hey, Joey, got blasted again, huh? Man, you look terrible! When you gonna learn? Now, lookit . . . you don't even have a pen or paper."

B. "Here, Joey. Need some paper? I have an extra pen, too. I know, I know. Another wild weekend. I had a wild time, too—only it was with pizza and videos and a crazy youth group. One of these days I'm gonna talk ya into trying it *my* way, OK?"

Hope you chose the second re-

sponse. If so, you're letting Joey know you *care* without putting him *down*. You've also given him something to think about without being pushy. Now you can pray that the Lord will continue to give you opportunities to reflect his love to Joey.

See how you're *reaching out* without becoming *intimate?* You're "in" the world but not "of" it. (See the next chapter for the scoop on being one *with* people without being one *of* them.)

Focus on the Real Issue

Remember when the lame man's friends broke through the roof and brought their pal to Jesus? (For a quick refresher, check out Luke 5:19-26.) Jesus didn't let them down. He physically healed the guy. But he also knew there were other issues going on in his life that were even more important than having bum legs.

Jesus took a deeper look. He saw *inside* the man. He knew the guy wasn't happy . . . and it wasn't just from not being able to play football. Jesus knew that the man's misery and loneliness came from being separated from his heavenly Father. So Jesus healed him *spiritually* as well. He forgave his sins and gave him new life.

In other words, he dealt with the

outside stuff . . . but focused a little deeper on the *real* issues that were troubling the paralytic.

When your friends brag about their sexual escapades, the party scene, or how much they get away with under their parents' noses . . . that's the *outside* stuff. The *real issue* is the INSIDE stuff . . . the "why" of what they're doing.

They're going too far with their girl/boyfriend because they're looking for love. If they knew *God's* love they'd have what they're searching for.

They're partying hearty and hardy because they have no purpose in life. Anything that feels good for the moment is attractive since they have nothing to make them feel good enough to last for eternity.

You know better. You know that deep inside they're lonely and miserable and lost because they don't know Christ as their best friend and Savior like *you* do. So instead of talking about what they're doing on the *outside* . . . try to deal with what's happening on the *inside*.

Karla is bragging about her date with Mitch. She confides in you that they went too far . . . but she did it because she's afraid of losing him. How will you respond?

A. "Karla, that was really stupid! Weren't you even thinking about STDs, pregnancy, or AIDS? You're only fifteen . . . you think he's gonna stick with you forever? No way."

B. "How do you feel about going too far? Guilty? Scared? Pressured? Proud? Karla, *no one* should pres-

132

Reflecting . . .

1 What Scriptures would help remind you to be "in" the world, but not a part "of" it?

2 What situations would you definitely stay out of?

3 Why are these situations different for different Christians?

sure you into doing something you're not comfortable with. You say you're scared of losing him . . . why? Because you feel more secure when he's around? Because you're scared of being alone? Those are *inside* reasons that would make a lot of people *respond outwardly* to things they really don't want to do. Can we talk more about it later?"

Again, I hope you selected the last response. By saying what you did, you've caused Karla to do some heavy thinking. Pray that Christ will help her keep an open mind. She'd be an excellent candidate to come to youth group when you have a special series on sex and dating.

Yes, God wants us to reach those who don't know him. But he *doesn't* want us to identify so closely with them that we're affected by their life-style.

Prayer: **Father, help me to learn how to be "in" the world but not "of" the world. I'm trusting your Holy Spirit to teach me the difference. Give me a genuine burden for those around me who don't know you. And help me not to condemn them for the wrong stuff they do, but teach me to love in spite of. I want to see them through *your* eyes . . . so I can keep my focus on the** ● *real* **issue: what's inside. *Amen.***

Choose Your Own Break... Sort Of

Didja know it's not 2 early 2 start hinting around 'bout whatcha want 4 Christmas? Here R our suggestions:

1. *Getting Ready for the Guy/Girl Thing* by Greg Johnson and Susie Shellenberger (Funny stuff. Meaty stuff. Stuff you *gotta* know about the opposite sex!)

2. A magazine subscription to *Brio* (for teen girls) or *Breakaway* (for teen guys). Hey, they're monthly mags and only $15 for a whole year! Where *else* ya gonna get the straight scoop on the hottest, the latest, and the best?

    What do Candace Cameron, Carl Lewis, Michael Chang, Michael W. Smith, DC Talk, Kevin Johnson, Stephen Curtis Chapman, Miss America, Carman, Kirk Cameron, and Chelsea Noble have in common? They've all been inside the pages of *Brio* or *Breakaway.* Now, doncha wish *you* had it? You can! Place an order right now: 1-800-A-FAMILY (but ask your folks 1st . . . $15 isn't cheap).

3. Another copy of *this* book (so you can give it 2 a friend!)

4. A set of Legos (Yeah, we know it's stupid. We want U-2 like the 1st 3 suggestions the best.)

One with, Not One Of

Jesus had an incredible skill: he could hang around the lowest of sinners and not be influenced by them. He spent time with tax collectors, prostitutes, radical revolutionaries ("zealots" who would just as soon murder a Roman as look at them), and thieves. He would even have hung around with you and me. We're the types who don't look too bad on the outside because we've learned how to hide most of our sins from everyone (except God, of course).

Jesus had the ability to be **one *with* people, without being one *of* them.** That is, when he spent time with "lowlifes" he didn't judge or condemn. He didn't even feel insecure or uncomfortable around them. (He had a slight advantage here in that he also *made* these folks.)

Glance around the hallways and you'll notice the partiers, girls and guys with "reputations," and tons of others who wear T-shirts, tops, skirts, and jewelry that you won't find in the average Sunday school. It's not easy to relate to these

135

people. Not only do they look and act different from you, but their language might be a little "saltier" than the dinner conversation in your home. How do you reach these people?

Well, you pierce your ear in four different places, buy a heavy-metal T-shirt with satanic signs on it, and shave the left side of your head . . . NOT!

Most folks who act or look different aren't too impressed with those who try to look the way they do . . . just to be in their group. They're more interested in *your response and attitude* toward their looks and actions. They may not want you to be in their group, but they'll notice if you treat them with respect, are kind to them . . . even talk to them like you would if they looked "normal."

Being "one *with*" someone means treating them the way Jesus would.

Jesus wasn't shocked or appalled at the behavior of those around him. He knew better than anyone that people who are separated from God are sometimes going to act like it; they may even *look* like it, too (whatever that means). Yet that didn't scare him away from accepting them—sin and all—and doing what he could to point them in the right direction.

While you may never be ultra-best friends with anyone who isn't a Christian (and a few churches even discourage *contact* with those who aren't), we think it's a great idea to practice what we call "normal Christian skills": acceptance, forgiveness, kindness, and love—all wrapped around the attitude that God created even the worst of sinners for a reason. They deserve to be treated well by at least one Christian so they can get an accurate picture of how Jesus would treat them.

Being Different Makes a Difference!

South Oak's gymnasium was filled with a mixture of sweat and popcorn smells and uncontrolled exhilaration. Less than twenty seconds remained in the last game of the season. The players couldn't even hear Coach Marston blaring instructions from the sidelines; the roar of the student body was too loud.

The band played the familiar school fight song while eight energetic cheerleaders led the crowd in one cheer after another. South Oak High School trailed by one, and two starters had fouled out earlier in the quarter.

Coach Marston called time-out and grabbed Shane. "Get the ball to Ryan as quickly as you can. It's not too late! We can still pull this one off."

Shane and Ryan were a team

within a team. Watching the two high-school juniors on the basketball court was like watching poetry in motion. They always seemed to be a step ahead of the rest of the players.

They'd pass the ball around to

other teammates, but it was obvious they had more ability than anyone else on the entire squad. Now that every second counted, it was no wonder Coach Marston tossed teamwork out the window and told them to "do their thing."

The buzzer sounded and the game was in motion once again. The opposing team started down the court with the ball. As Coach Marston barked out defensive instructions from the sidelines, Shane stabbed for the ball with his lightning reflexes and miraculously stole it from the frustrated Eagle guard. Almost as if he had read Shane's mind, Ryan was already headed down the court waiting for Shane's pass.

Now with just eight seconds left on the clock, Ryan raced past two defenders to the hoop. With two seconds remaining, Shane lofted a pass to the basket, and Ryan rammed the ball through the hoop as the final buzzer sounded South Oak's dramatic victory!

Almost immediately the team was mobbed with friends, family members, and local newspaper sports photographers.

"Time to celebrate!" Mike yelled to his teammates as he joined the massive celebration on the gym floor.

"Party!" joined Ryan.

The locker room buzzed with plans for the night.

"Who's grabbing the 'brew'?"

"My older bro's meeting us at Kwik Stop in half an hour. He said if we won tonight, the first three six-packs are on him," announced Chad.

"All right!"

"What a guy!"

"Yeah, and he also said if we'll meet him outside the store with our money, he'll get everything else we want."

"What are we waiting for? Let's get outta here!"

"Yeah! We got some serious partying to do!"

"Hey, Shane! Why don't you loosen up for once and come with us this time?" invited Mike.

"Yeah, Shane. It's time you *really* became part of the team," pressed Ryan.

"C'mon, guys, you know I don't drink."

"So what? Just come and have fun with the rest of us. You don't have to drink," Ryan continued.

"I can think of better things to do than watching you guys fall all over each other," Shane laughed. "You can tell me all about it on Monday . . . the part you're able to remember, that is. Catch you later!"

Reaching Out

Shane waited until Saturday afternoon to give Ryan a call. "How you doing, Ry?"

"Uhhh," he moaned. "Can you come over? I wanna talk."

"Sure, but it doesn't sound like you're in the best of shape right now. Are you sure this is a good time?"

"No, it's not a good time, but I want to talk to you anyway. Please, Shane. Just come over."

Shane placed the receiver in its cradle and headed toward Ryan's. As he heard his screen door slam, he couldn't help but remember all the great times they'd had the past five years. He smiled as he recalled their first meeting on the baseball field in the Blue Tigers Little League. Ryan had his cap on backward: his symbol of doing things "his way." They had collided during practice when both were going for a fly ball. Even though their white practice pants were covered with dirt and grass stains, the boys laughed hysterically. That day marked the beginning of a close friendship.

The following year, Ryan's family moved into a neighborhood in Shane's school district, and the two had become even closer. Though Ryan sometimes accepted his invitation to attend church, Shane was still praying that he'd become a Christian.

As he turned the corner to drive the last five blocks to Downing Street, he remembered how close Ryan had been to making a spiritual decision last summer when he had agreed to attend church camp. Though he was desperately interested in knowing God better, it was obvious something was still holding him back.

Now, as they were in the middle of their junior year, Shane worried that he was completely losing Ryan to the party scene. It had become a Friday night ritual for the rest of the team to get drunk after every game—whether they won or not. Ryan had fallen prey to the pressure.

As he shut the car door and climbed the porch steps, Shane wondered what he could say this time that he hadn't already said before.

A Listening Friend

He found Ryan in his bedroom with the curtains drawn and the lights off, obviously experiencing a major hangover. Shane sat on the floor beside the bed and spoke softly.

"You look awful!"

"Tell me something I *don't* know!" Ryan responded. "Someone slipped some 'X' in my drink last night. Ohhh. My insides feel like they've been ripped apart with a lawn mower."

Shane didn't know a lot about "X," other than the fact it was short for "ecstasy" and was a powerful and popular drug making the rounds at his high school. "Ry, do you really think it's worth it? I mean, look at you!"

"That's what I want to talk to you about. Shane, I've known you for a long time. No matter how many times I've screwed up, you've remained a real friend."

"Hey, listen—"

"No. You listen! I know I'm not in real good shape right now, but I do know what I'm talking about. You've always been a good guy. The only reason I started partying was because I couldn't say no to the pressure. I just wanted to be included, you know?"

"I hear you."

"But—you never gave in. Everyone knows what you stand for; they know how involved you are in your church and youth group. And most of the times I've gone with you, I've really enjoyed it. I've come real close several times to making a commitment to God, but something always holds me back."

"I know. I've sensed that."

"I want what you have, Shane. I need that strength. I don't want to keep giving in to the pressure of things that I really don't even want to do."

"Ryan, that's great!" Shane yelled. As Ryan covered his ears and winced in pain, Shane remembered he should keep the volume down.

"Hold on," Ryan continued. "I *want* to give my life to Christ . . . but

I'm scared. And you can't tell anybody I said that!"

"C'mon, Ry! I'm your friend, remember?"

"Yeah, yeah. Guess I'm just scared of all I know I'll have to give up to become a Christian."

Counting the Cost

"Listen to me," Shane began. "All the things you'll give up to follow the Lord are the very same things that are ruining your life. You really don't want to do them anyway. You said that yourself."

When Ryan didn't respond, Shane continued, "It just makes sense to give your life to God. It's obvious you're miserable. You already said you need God's strength to say no to the things you don't want to do."

"Yeah, I know," Ryan agreed.

"But you're right in thinking about the cost," Shane continued. "Following Jesus isn't always easy. It means saying no to some attractive things everyone else seems to be doing. And they'll probably give you a hard time about it, too. But, hey, look who God's given you for a friend!"

"Get off it!" Ryan smiled, as he tossed a pillow at Shane's head. "Everything you're saying makes a lot of sense. I really want to do this. I *need* to do this. But I'm still scared."

Shane smiled and breathed a

prayer for help as he leaned forward and pulled his pocket-sized New Testament out of his jacket.

Life-Style Evangelism

Shane's life opened the door for Ryan's salvation. Within his life-style, he also held three important aspects of leading someone to Christ. Let's sneak a peek at Shane's secrets. Life-style evangelism for him meant:

1. Friendship. By being a friend to Ryan, Shane had earned the right to be heard. He had taken the time to establish rapport. Their friendship spanned five years. They had shared baseball, basketball, camping, and several other common interests. By simply being a *friend* to Ryan over the years, Shane had earned his respect and won his trust.

2. Consistency. Shane was consistent. First of all, he was consistent in his friendship with Ryan. He continued to encourage him and kept the lines of communication open, even when Ryan drifted into other areas. He wasn't condemning, yet he clearly didn't condone Ryan's actions either.

Chances are your non-Christian friend already knows what's *wrong* in his life. Instead of focusing on those wrongs, continue to love him and make it clear you want him involved in your youth group. Invite him often and encourage his attendance. When he *does* come, make him feel loved and accepted by introducing him to your church friends.

Shane was also consistent in his walk with Christ. It would have been easy to accept the invitation to the party and simply not drink once he arrived. But Shane knew his impact would eventually be stronger if he didn't attend the party at all.

He took a strong stand for what he believed was right. This made it absolutely clear in Ryan's mind that *compromise* was not an option. Because of Shane's consistency in avoiding evil, Ryan was able to better discern the difference between Shane's life and the lives of their other friends. He eventually came to the conclusion that he wanted that difference.

Many times Christian teens rationalize and think, *It'll be a good witness to attend the party and not drink. Then everyone will know I'm a Christian and can actually see me taking a stand.* But the next day at school when the hallway gossip floats through the tiles and someone's naming off everyone who attended the party, they won't take the time to stop and say, "Oh, yeah, but I don't think she drank anything." Your name will simply be remembered as one among many who attended the party. Guaranteed!

What kind of witness is that? Surprise! Your non-Christian friends see it as one big inconsistency. They don't want to see how similar you can be to them; if you're claiming to be a Christian, they want to see the *difference!*

3. Love. First Corinthians 13 tells us that love is patient. Ryan had come close to making a spiritual commitment several times. When he didn't make a commit- ▼ ment at last summer's camp, Shane might have been tempted to respond, "What *is* it with you, Ryan? I give up!" but he didn't. He continued to love his friend and realized he needed to be patient.

At a luncheon held at Azusa Pacific University on February 7, 1990, Tony Campolo addressed a crowd of professors and students. Commenting on personal evangelism, he told of asking a crowd of ten thousand how they were won to the Lord.

Reflecting . . .

1 Susie mentioned "patience." What are some other characteristics of love from 1 Corinthians 13 that will positively impact the lives of your friends?

2 What person had the biggest impact on your becoming a Christian? What was it about this person's life-style that attracted you to Christ?

3 How does the quality of your own life-style measure up in terms of friendship, consistency, and love toward others?

4 This will take some courage: Talk to a friend or youth minister and have them give you honest feedback on how well you demonstrate Christ-likeness through your life-style. Ask them to tell you what both your strengths and weaknesses are.

When he asked how many came to know Jesus Christ through television evangelism, no one raised a hand. When he asked how many were won to the Lord through evangelistic tracts, no hands were raised. When he asked how many became Christians through radio ministry, he saw four hands go up. When he inquired as to how many were won through a great sermon, he counted forty hands.

When he finally asked, "How many of you came to know Jesus Christ personally because someone locked on to you and wouldn't let you go?" a sea of hands all over the auditorium were raised.

What does that tell us about evangelism? When our life is truly different it will make a difference in those around us.

Should You Be a Christian Punching Bag?

Dear Greg:

I've been trying to witness to my friends about Christ, but I'm always being made fun of or called "Preacher Boy." At first I tried to ignore it, but now it's beginning to hurt. There's no one at school to talk to because I'm the only Christian willing to tell others about him in my grade. What can I do?

FESTUS, MISSOURI

I want to compliment you on being willing to "take a licking and keep on ticking" for the Savior. But I sense the continual pounding is getting to you—big time.

While there are a variety of ways to witness to others about your faith, teens are most skeptical—and cruel—when it comes to "overly vocal" religious classmates, especially if you're trying to witness to a

group. It's easy for people to ridicule you when they've lost their identity in a crowd. They can feed on each other's jokes and taunts and not feel guilty because they think *it's the group, not just me.*

With teens especially, you have

BAPPITY!
BAPPITY!
BAP!

145

to "win the right to be heard." That is, your friends want to *see* a sermon before they *hear* one. They don't care how much you know, until they know how much you care. You have to take the man out of the ghetto before you can take the ghetto out of the man. (OK, enough cliches!) You get the picture. *Actions speak louder than words.*

A better strategy is to let your *life* do the talking.

I (Greg) wasn't a Christian in high school, and I remember the people I *didn't* want to be like: the religious-sounding churchgoers. I didn't understand what they were talking about. And I thought that if I ever became a churchgoer, then I'd have to be just like them! Plus, I was very insecure and would have never had the courage to change groups—especially to join a group (or a belief) that others put down.

While *your* personality fits *you,* many others aren't attracted to vocal Christians.

Why? Two reasons:

1. It's easy to feel guilty around vocal Christians. Usually, even a non-Christian *knows* when their behavior doesn't measure up. Instead of looking to Someone who can take their guilt away, many people just bury it deeper and build their shell a little stronger. People don't like to feel bad—and guilt makes them feel bad.

2. Vocal Christians sometimes (though not always) seem judgmental or condemning. *Holier than thou* is the phrase that may be going through a non-Christian's mind. Even someone who isn't a Christian knows no one is any better than they are (and they're right!). When someone confronts their behavior or beliefs, it's easy for them to say, "What makes you think you're so much better than me?"

I don't know what you're saying when you share your faith with friends at school, but the key is those three words: *share your faith.* It means "offer something you believe," not "confront them on their un-Christian behavior." People who don't know Christ have every excuse to act like it—and most of the time they will. They don't have the Holy Spirit inside to help strengthen and remind them to do right. When you're carrying around a dump truck full of sin, it's easier to add to the load . . . especially when you're not looking to get rid of it.

If sharing your faith means offering something you believe, then the recipient should have at least some interest in receiving it. **Live a**

life that's different. It's how you treat *them* and *others* that will prompt people to ask you what you've got.

When I finally got away from my "friends" at school and heard the gospel for the first time, I remembered those who lived their faith. They were the first people I told. When I got around to telling my old high-school buddies, they weren't interested in hanging around me anymore. It hurt, but I wasn't dependent on their friendship to sur-

vive. I knew where to find better friends because acquaintances who were Christians had accepted me, no matter what my behavior (and it wasn't very good).

If God's telling you to be vocal with your faith no matter how ridiculed you are (and he may be), do it. It is possible to be vocal about your faith without being a turnoff. But another good action plan is to work on being an unusually good friend to people and wait to share with them when they show an interest.

Reflecting . . .

1 What goes through your mind when someone is overtly vocal with their faith around non-Christians?

2 What kind of people are exciting to be around when they're sharing their faith?

3 What's the difference?

What's Wrong with This Picture?

Dear Greg:

I have this friend who's not a Christian. I've been trying to think of ways to help introduce him to the Christian faith, but have come up short in trying to think of any good ones. Now, I realize that he's 17, and trying to convert him from atheism would be challenging. I'd at least like to influence him as best as I can in the next year or so before he leaves for college.

CEDARBURG, WISCONSIN

Though you don't give any clues how close a friend this guy is, I'll assume he's more than an acquaintance you don't know that well. It seems like you really care for him.

I think you're right about the challenge you're up against, too. If he says he's an atheist, it means he wants to let you know he's going to be a hard nut to crack.

A lot of people become atheists because they figure if God is like the picture they have in their mind, they would just as soon believe in nothing. Here are ten pictures

people have of God. All are common misconceptions of who he really is. I've included some Scripture references that may help clear up some of these wrong pictures.

God Is a Churchgoer

God's dressed up with no place to go, so he heads off to a funny-shaped building to spout forth words that are hard to understand. If people want to, they can contact him there. Otherwise, he's out of reach. (See Psalm 139:7-12.)

God Is a Baptist

God has been squeezed into the mold of a certain denomination that's an easy target for ridicule. (Actually, since all churches are made up of humans, they're *all* easy targets.) People who have this picture of God disagree with a certain portion of the church's beliefs, so along with discarding the church, they discard God. (See 1 Corinthians 1:10-12 and Matthew 7:1-2.)

God Is a Nice Old Man

He's got a long white beard, but is way out of touch with our fast-paced society. His book is old, his commandments are old, the people who go to his church are old . . . *he's* old. He's more like Santa Claus. When you really want something (like to get out of trouble), and if you're good

enough, he'll give it to you. This kind of God is powerless to really understand us. (See John 16:23-24 and Hebrews 13:8.)

God's a GIANT Cop

He sits behind heavenly billboards waiting to catch people who are having too much fun. (See John 10:10 and Acts 3:19.)

God's an Antique

He's been inherited from our parents, passed down from generation to generation. We know about him because we live in a house that rewards the right talk. But in our minds, God is a relic of the past. He's not relevant for today and probably isn't that interested in our problems. (See 1 Peter 5:7 and Romans 8:16-17.)

God Is a WASP (White, Anglo-Saxon, Protestant)

Or at least an American. This God is tightly duct-taped to our culture, politics, or skin color. He looks with more interest on us than the other "inferior" classes or nationalities. (See Colossians 3:11 and 2 Peter 3:9.)

God Is Religious

He's only interested in spiritual things like praying, Bible memorization, hymns, witnessing, etc. If you don't perform in some spiritual way, you probably can't merit his attention or love. (See Matthew 6:25-34.)

God Is a Crutch

We go to this God when we're in trouble. Therefore, those who go to him must be so weak they can't handle their own problems. He's there to escape to in order to bolster our feelings of security. (See Luke 9:23 and Romans 12:11.)

God Is a Belief

He—or it!—is an abstract philosophical concept that you can make into whatever you want. Everyone has some sort of "God-consciousness," so that means everyone can contact him on their own. (See John 10:27-30.)

God Is a Big Disappointment

Since he did such a bad job with my body, home life, athletic ability, brain, dating life, etc., he just must

not be real. If he's really God, then why is there death, disease, famine, war, and suffering? This concept leads many to say "I've tried it, and it doesn't work. He's wronged me in the past (or wronged someone I know); therefore, he can't be trusted." (See Philippians 1:20-21.)

When someone doesn't have an accurate picture of who God really is and what he wants, naturally they're not going to trust him with their lives. Frankly, if I believed any of these things about God, I wouldn't want to hang around with him either!

The only clear picture we have of God comes to us in the person of Jesus Christ.

The Son is the radiance of God's glory and the exact representation of his being, sustaining all things by his powerful word. After he had provided purification

151

Reflecting . . .

1 Which picture do most of your non-Christian friends have of Christ?

2 Look up the passage after each "wrong picture," and write down the real truth.

for sins, he sat down at the right hand of the Majesty in heaven. (Hebrews 1:3)

People will measure their view of God by everything except the truth. Naturally, that's Satan's strategy. If he can focus someone's eyes on the wrong type of God, people will reject the true God.

That's why as you seek to influence your friend, the best idea is to challenge him on the *life of* ● *Christ.* Don't talk church, rules, commandments, his behavior, hypocrites . . . *anything* except Jesus Christ. Give him a New Testament he can understand, and ask him to read one chapter a day and write down the questions he comes up with. While he may not respond throughout his remaining high-school months, at least you've given him the right foundation to build on.

152

Have You Got the Right Picture?

The last chapter talked about helping a friend get the right picture of God. That way, they'll be responding to the real thing, not some imaginary god who doesn't exist.

But what about you?

We know a lot of Christians who don't share their faith because they've got some wrong ideas, too. Here are a few:

The Pollyanna Syndrome

Pollyanna, of course, was a character in a book and a Disney movie who always saw the positive instead of the negative. Though that's not a bad idea in general, a "Christian Pollyanna" thinks believers aren't ever supposed to have problems. Then when they *do* struggle, they think there's something wrong with *them,* that their faith is somehow inadequate compared to others. Consequently, they never feel comfortable sharing Christ because they just don't measure up.

If *you* believe Christians don't have problems, one verse should shoot down that idea quick.

I have told you these things, so that in me you may have peace. In this world you will have trouble. But take heart! I have overcome the world. (John 16:33)

Two things:

First, don't ever believe that since you're a Christian you won't face tough times. That's La La Land, and you shouldn't go there.

Second, don't ever tell anyone that becoming a Christian will solve all their problems. In fact, it will sometimes create more problems than it solves. But at least they'll have the promise in the first half of that passage—PEACE.

God-Loves-Me-More Disease

Raise your right hand and repeat after us:

I'm one of five billion people who live on planet Earth.

Jesus Christ suffered separation from God so that each one of those five billion wouldn't have to.

God does *not* play favorites.

I am no better or worse than anyone else who has ever lived.

Being a Christian does not put me in a heavenly club here on earth.

It only means I agree with *God's plan* of salvation.

Amen.

The moment you start believing you're actually better than other people is the moment God quits using you to help others find him.

I-Know-I'm-Not-Perfect-But-Other-Christians-Should-Be Disorder

It's a discouraging fact: Christians sometimes hurt other Christians. For the person who has been on the receiving end of that hurt, it can be devastating and demoralizing. Some keep their faith only because they want heaven. They naturally hold back in sharing their faith because they don't really believe a Christian is all that different than others.

Well, they're right!

Every Christian, at one time or another, has let another Christian down. Sometimes in a big way. Perhaps their churchgoing parents got a divorce. Their youth leader left his wife and ran off with one of the female sponsors. Or maybe the friend who led them to Christ was seen drinking at a party.

Sadly, Christians—even "mature" Christians—make big mistakes that hurt others. It's discouraging, to say the least. It makes you wonder if this Jesus stuff is all true. And it causes you to rethink whether it's a good idea to even mention *anything* about your faith.

One bummer about being a Christian for a long time is seeing people you trusted let you down. But count on it. It's going to happen sometime in your life. The only consolation you have is realizing that that person isn't Jesus. He or she didn't do miracles, say incredibly true stuff—or die for you. Satan will use their failures to keep you from staying in the battle. Don't let him. Instead, learn from their mistakes and never put all of your faith in the example of another forgiven sinner. They'll eventually let you down.

You'll-Never-Doubt Condition

While some have been given the gift of never having second thoughts about all they've been taught, many of us haven't. God understands we're human, and he knows it's tough to throw our lives into something we don't always completely understand. So he's never intimidated by honest questions. In fact, he welcomes them.

He knows that your struggle to grasp all of the elements of faith in him will help others who are struggling, too.

In Acts 17, Paul went to a city called Berea. These folks wouldn't just take everything he said at face value. Though "they received the message with great eagerness," they also "examined the Scriptures every day to see if what Paul said was true" (Acts 17:11).

What a great example to follow! Eagerness, followed by an honest search.

Don't believe that Christians can't doubt or have questions about their faith. And don't tell someone you're trying to share your faith with that they have to believe everything you say. Both of you should take your doubts and questions to the Bible. In every *essential* question you or they have, it has the answer. (Dinosaurs, nuclear fusion, and why girls go to the bathroom in groups not included.)

--- Reflecting . . . ---

1 Since you want to see Christ as clearly as possible, what can you do to bring your picture of him into better focus?

2 Name some other misconceptions Christians have about the faith.

How to Tell When a Friend Is Ready

Is it better to drop a "gospel bomb" on a friend or wait for the right time?

If you don't look at people as "projects," and you're not getting a free meal at McDonald's from your youth leader for leading someone to Christ, then it's always better to wait for the right time. Some people just aren't ready to make a spiritual change.

Here are a few reasons why people procrastinate about giving their lives to God, and how you can respond:

They're Not Ready

They're not ready to believe that Jesus Christ actually rose from the dead. This is the major issue for people who are genuinely searching. They can't get themselves to believe in something as miraculous as the Resurrection. One idea to ▼

speed up that process is to show them the Old Testament Scriptures that predict aspects of Christ's life and death. Then from the New Testament, show them how he fulfilled those prophecies. (See "Stuff at the End of the Book #3," on page 205).

Going through these passages may move them another notch toward believing it's true. But what may move them up even faster is rubbing shoulders with others who have obviously been changed. Your testimony, or those of others in your church or town, will often point to one conclusion: only a God who is living today could have changed their life.

They Still Have a Few Questions

They may not even know what they are yet, but they know something's holding them back.

Whenever they're in a situation (church, youth group, or a special big event) where they hear something about God or the Bible, afterwards, make sure you ask if they have any questions. If you can answer them, fine. If not, write down their question and find the answer for them later.

Patience really is the key. Hurrying someone or pressing for a decision benefits no one. Yes, there are some who have heard everything backwards and forwards, who understand the gospel and who think it's right—but they just can't decide. Occasionally, these folks *do* need to be asked, "Wouldn't today be a good day to become a Christian?" But most often, it's better to wait until they're completely ready.

They Fear Losing Other Friends

They're afraid their friends may drop them if they start to get "religious."

This person is in the counting-the-cost stage. They're looking at a potential negative that would change their circle of friends or routine. They're not ready. What they don't know, of course, is that when you become a Christian, you get a gigantic family of new, hopefully better friends. The best strategy is to wait and let them discern for themselves who would make a better quality friend.

One objection we often hear is that a youth group is "cliquish." People who are already "in" don't like letting others in. They're safe and secure with the group and often fail to treat outsiders warmly. If your group is like that, you may be fighting an uphill battle. Try the strategy below, and don't bring friends to youth group until you feel they will be welcomed.

They Don't Understand That It's a Relationship

A lot of people don't understand the difference between *religion* and *relationship*. Most pre-Christians feel that Christianity is just like every other religion: obey a set of rules, do the right "spiritual things," and you'll go to heaven. Actually, becoming a Christian is admitting

How to "De-clique" Your Youth Group

- Talk with your youth leader or sponsors. Let them know you'd like to invite a friend to the group, but that you're afraid others won't accept them. Suggest that your leader present a series of discussions or talks on this subject.

- Make sure you're not part of the problem. Whether you're shy or outgoing, there are things you can do to make others feel welcome (e.g., greet new people instead of just talking to your own friends; ask them questions that will make them feel like somebody paid attention to them; and, if you bring someone, introduce them to a few friends one-on-one, not the whole group).

- Talk to a few of your close friends in the group, and ask what they think. If they agree the group is too cliquish, then all of you can start being more friendly to new-comers.

- Send "thanks for coming" notes to people who visit Sunday school or youth group.

that we *can't* keep the rules (we're sinners) and believing that God provided a way to take care of our eternally fatal condition (which he did by allowing Jesus to die in our place). Our faith, therefore, is placed in a person, not a set of rules. We become a child of God (John 1:12), not a guilt-ridden zombie trying to follow a code.

Whenever they use the term *religion* (which means, "man's search for God"), gently inform them of the difference. If you want your friends to get an accurate picture of what it's like to follow God, they must see it as a relationship, not rules. After all, Christianity isn't a *religion*, it's a way of life!

Their Parents Would Never Let Them Go to Church

Many parents are very hostile toward church or anything that has to do with religion. If that's the case with one of your friends, don't force the issue. (Remember the story about Debbie in chapter 22? Susie was pushy, but in a fun way. And she never tried to get Deb to disobey her parents, but continued encouraging her to keep the subject *open* with her folks.) After all, it's *fellowship* with other believers that a seeker or a new Christian needs, not just to be inside a church building. Hang close with him, give a tape, or open the Bible with him during lunch or after school.

While it would be great if he had his parents' support, these days, that's not always the case.

One more thing: don't ever try to pull one over on the parents. They *will* find out, and they'll likely clamp down even harder. Besides that, it's wrong.

It's Not the Right Time Yet

Perhaps no one is adequately able to help root them deeper in the faith, so God is not letting them respond yet.

You could be doing everything right—being a great friend, taking them to youth group, Campus Life, or Young Life, answering their questions, giving them great Christian tapes . . . and maybe they're still not ready. Always remember: God is just as concerned about after-care as he is about birth. He may know that no one will be able to help root them as a

new believer, so he's waiting for a more opportune time to prompt them to respond. Someone once said to me, "If you save them, you've got to keep them. If God saves them, it's his responsibility." Wait for God's timing.

As much fun as it is to see someone enter the kingdom, it's even more rewarding to see them still tracking for the Lord many years later. If God can be patient, so can you.

The Bible Still Looks Too Confusing, Boring, and Big

Hopefully, you or an older Christian friend have taken thirty minutes to explain the Bible to a "seeking" friend. People who haven't grown up with it in their home (and even some who have) are right when they say it's big and confusing (but definitely not boring!). Here are a few things to cover with someone when

---

Reflecting . . .

1 What are some other reasons why people don't come to Christ?

2 Can you think of other ways to "de-clique" your youth group?

they're ready to start checking out God's Word for themselves:

- Explain the difference between the Old Testament and the New Testament.
- Talk about the Gospels (Matthew, Mark, Luke, and John) and the life of Christ. Keep them focused on Jesus.
- Let them know that the rest of the New Testament is basically letters written by Christian leaders . . . to other Christians to cover specific things that were happening in the church. Some they'll be able to understand, but others they won't until they know who wrote it, to whom they wrote it, and why they wrote it.
- Give them the twenty-eight-day challenge: Read one chapter from Matthew each day (have them skip the genealogy). That will allow God's Word to do the convincing instead of you.

When the Good News Is Not Good News

OK, let's make a list of all the stuff you have as a Christian:

- You have a personal God living inside you who's intimately interested in every area of your life.
- You have forgiveness from your sin and freedom from guilt.
- You have peace in the midst of trials.
- You have a Friend when you're lonely.
- You have hope when everything seems hopeless.
- You have a joy just knowing you're alive and loved unconditionally.
- You have bread to give away to people who are starving—the message of eternal life to offer those who are heading to eternal separation from God.

WOW! This GOOD NEWS really is **GREAT NEWS!**

With all this, it ought to be easy to let others know just how *good* this news really is, right?

You tell us.

No matter how great this news

CHRISTIAN CHECKLIST

☑ PERSONAL GOD
☑ PEACE
☑ CONSTANT FRIEND
☑ HOPE
☑ JOY
☑ BREAD

is, there are ways *Christians* are making this good news BAD NEWS. No, they don't do it intentionally—they're just not aware that hardened hearts will find any excuse to stay that way.

Here are a few ways Christians turn the GOOD NEWS into BAD NEWS:

Focusing on Nonessentials

The Good News is not good news when we lay "nonessential" rules on the backs of new Christians or those considering Christ.

Right behavior is important, true. But when we emphasize behavior before the person of Jesus Christ, it's bad news. Jesus doesn't tell anyone to clean up their life before they come to him. The woman caught in the act of adultery was first forgiven by Jesus before he gave her the challenge of "Go, and sin no more." What he was saying was go and quit being a prostitute—an obvious wrong behavior that would have been a constant source of guilt (John 8:1-11).

Godly living is a process we're all involved with. Some will be able to quit bad behavior right away (drugs or drinking). For others, it will take time to get rid of habits that need to be weeded out (swearing, smoking, anger).

When talking to someone about becoming a Christian, don't even ▼

mention that they'll need to change things like: hair length or style, clothes, jewelry, musical tastes, smoking, swearing, movies they go to—anything that is an outward sign of rebellion or habits formed in ignorance. The goal is to present Jesus and let *him* do the changing from the *inside out*. That's the only way long-term change occurs: He must first take up residence and begin to clean house—and he'll do it at a pace he knows that person can handle.

We shouldn't tell someone to clean up their act before they come to Christ. They don't have the **power** to do it—because they don't have the Holy Spirit within—or the **reason** to try—why try to please God by living a life of obedience when you don't know him? (See Acts 15.)

Failing to Back Up Words with Action

The Good News is not good news when it comes from someone whose life—most of the time—doesn't back up his words.

Does that mean you have to be perfect before you can begin sharing your faith? Hardly. God specializes in using forgiven sinners still moving toward a more godly life in order to spread his love. Since no one's perfect, this fact is obvious.

But someone trying to live on

both sides of the fence is another matter. A Christian who drinks or takes drugs even semi-regularly is a hypocrite, plain and simple. If they try to share their faith with someone at school and that person knows they're a partier, the gospel will taste very bad. Though a friend may not say it, they'll think, *If that's what being a Christian really means, I guess I don't have to change.* (See Acts 4:1-14.)

Presenting Logical Arguments Only

The Good News is not good news when the gospel is hidden in "intellectualism" instead of a choice of lordship.

While a couple of friends may be "logically convinced" about the facts of Jesus and the Bible, most won't turn to Christ on facts alone. Why? Because becoming a Christian means letting someone else run their life.

When you share your faith with a friend, please, present all the facts as best as you know them (see "Stuff at the End of the Book #2, Your Most Important Relationship," on page 201), and ALSO let them know that God doesn't want to just be another piece of their life, he WANTS their life. Whenever we give something to God halfway, he doesn't really have room to work. He needs permission to have total control. (See Acts 17:18-33.)

I heard a speaker once tell his audience, "All God requires is that you give everything you know about yourself, to everything you know about Jesus."

Good advice.

Not Starting Where They Are

The Good News is not good news when we fail to begin at the spiritual starting point of those we're trying to reach.

A ton of stuff goes into a person's life and brain before you get to be their friend. Perhaps they've had a good life in a solid family, but just no church background. They're not opposed to becoming a Christian, they just don't know much about it. Maybe they went to church when they were little, but quit going.

Some have parents who've had a bad experience with a church, so they bad-mouth it whenever they can. Others have had a bad experience with Christians! (Yes, it happens all the time.)

When you begin a friendship with someone, you probably don't know the good or bad experiences they've had with church or with Christians. Maybe as you're walking or driving by a church you can try asking a few harmless questions:

- Has your family ever gone to church before? Was it good or bad? What do you think of it now?

- Have you ever tried to read the Bible? What did you think? (Depending on their response to these questions, you may be able to go a little deeper.)
- Who do you think Jesus is?
- What do you think it means to be a Christian? Have you ever thought about it?

Asking these types of questions will tell you verbally (their answers) and nonverbally (their facial expressions and body language when you ask them) what they know and how warm they might be to talking further. Plus, it will give you the chance to clear up any misconceptions or answer other questions that might come up. Because there is no pressure to "lead them to Christ," it should be pretty relaxed.

With some friends, it's even a good idea to ask permission to respond to one of their statements: "That's an interesting view that God is everywhere and in everything. Where'd you come up with it? Would it be all right if I explained what the Bible says?"

Or one of their questions: "I'd like to answer that question you have about the Bible being full of contradictions. Would it be all right if we got together after school tomorrow (with my youth leader) to

see if we can find an answer?" Their response will tell you how serious they are about actually finding out the answer or hearing what you have to say.

By starting *where they are,* you help them make sense out of something that *could* be very confusing. Rarely would you want to open the conversation by talking about Communion or the sixteen people who got baptized at church last Sunday. Find out what they know and where they are first—then you'll know what to do. (See Acts 8:26-40.)

Failing to Emphasize the Essentials

The Good News is not good news when we fail to emphasize the resurrection of Christ and the importance of seeking forgiveness from God.

The unique part about the Christian faith that separates it from every other "religion" is this: We're the only ones who believe our leader is still alive! All other religions—Hindu, Muslim, Mormon, Jehovah's Witness, etc.—are living the way they do because a now-dead leader said to. Christ's resurrection is the difference and should therefore be emphasized.

Asking for forgiveness, or repenting, is also essential. If Jesus Christ is still alive . . . that makes him God! If *he's* God, we're not!

Realizing who God is should be very humbling. We can't come to

Christ and keep our pride up to guard us. We have to admit we fall short of his ideal; we need to believe that Jesus died to forgive us for our sinful nature; and we need to receive this gift (ask him for it) before he will come into our lives and give us eternal life. (See Acts 17:16-34.)

If our friends become Christians on their own terms, they will eventually bag it. The life of faith tells us that to please God, we "must believe that he exists and that he rewards those who earnestly seek him" (Hebrews 11:6). There's only room for one Lord, and that's Jesus.

Reflecting . . .

1 Can you identify a time in your own life when you reflected the "Good News" as "bad news?"

2 How else can Christians make the Good News *bad* news?

Four Things You Do with Mistakes

Mark had been a Christian for about five months. He was an extremely sensitive person and really wanted to do what God wanted him to. He read his Bible daily and went to church and a midweek Bible study for college guys. It seemed like he was on a fast track to spiritual maturity. I (Greg) felt certain God was going to use him for something big. I was wrong.

One day he phoned and said we needed to talk. We got together the next day.

"Greg, I don't think I'm going to make it with this Christian thing," he said. "I'll be at work, digging my irrigation ditches like normal, and I'll just start shaking. There are so many things I feel like I have to do to be the believer God wants me to that I can hardly sleep at night. Bad

thoughts come into my head that I know shouldn't be there, and I can't seem to get rid of them."

I tried to explain to Mark that Christians aren't perfect—that we still have tons of areas to change in—but that God is patient. He

169

knows (thank goodness) we can't do it all at once. We prayed, and then I suggested he cut back on some of his Christian commitments and just spend time in the Word. That seemed to help for a week or two, but then he'd get the shakes again because he always felt he was being disobedient in some area.

He talked to his pastor, who, like me, continually emphasized God's grace and forgiveness no matter what we've done. There were many more long conversations, but about two months later, he chucked it all. He hasn't returned, either.

He Couldn't Believe One Truth

Mark's story is sad because he was never able to grasp this fact: God uses forgiven sinners—not perfect saints—to accomplish his will in the hearts of those around us.

All it takes is one quick read through the life of four biblical "heroes" to see that.

- King David committed adultery with Bathsheba, but God continued to use him (see 1 Samuel 11–12 and Psalm 51).
- Jonah tried to run away from God, had three days to "contemplate" his poor decision, wound up preaching to the people of Nineveh, then got

ticked off at God for being so forgiving to them (take ten minutes and read the four chapters in Jonah, then check out Susie's version of what happened in chapter 43—page 193).

- Moses was a murderer, yet God still used him to lead the nation of Israel as they went to the Promised Land (his story's in Exodus).
- Peter, one of Jesus' closest friends, denied he even knew Christ three times (read John 18:15-27; 21:15-19).

Does God use perfect people? NEVER! There ain't none!

The space shuttle is a multibillion dollar piece of machinery that has been fined-tuned to near-perfection. Do you know how it gets to its destination? It makes mistakes.

Huge planes carry hundreds of thousands of passengers to their destinations each day. Across the globe, only a handful of these giant jets crash each year. They truly are more safe than driving a car. How do they stay on course and make it to their final destination? They make mistakes.

Both the space shuttle and commercial jets have guidance devices that keep them on course through a series of mistakes. The automatic pilot system navigates the plane to-

170

ward a city, but the plane naturally drifts off-course (due to high winds and an extremely small amount of human error within the system). As soon as it drifts, the system pulls it back on course—until the next inevitable mistake.

The result: 99.99 percent of the time the plane reaches its correct destination.

Making Corrections

Throughout your life—including your teenage years—you'll make hundreds of mistakes. Some big, some small. Like Mark in the story from the beginning of the chapter, you may begin to wonder if you're really cut out to be a Christian. After all, aren't we supposed to be holy? Well, yes, but holiness is a lifetime goal, not an overnight achievement. And it can only be done through the Holy Spirit living within us. In other words, we can't live a godly life in our own strength. It's impossible. But guess what? God doesn't expect us to! He calls us to a life of holiness, then gives us the equipment we need to make it possible. The tool? The Holy Spirit. No one will be perfect like Jesus until we see him face to face (1 John 3:2-3). But he can perfect our *heart* before God if we allow him to have complete control.

While we each need to set our sights on becoming more like Jesus,

we must realize we're going to stray off course from time to time (actually, daily). That doesn't mean God is mad at us, hates us, and can't use us anymore. It just means we need to get back on course.

My old basketball coach taught me something about life I'll never forget. He said, "There are four things you do with a mistake if you're going to be successful in this sport":

1. **Recognize it**
2. **Admit it**
3. **Learn from it**
4. **Forget it**

"The great players," he said, "can do all four of those things in the span of about five seconds. If you let your mind dwell on that bad pass or a poor shot, you might as well come out of the game. You won't be doing the team any good."

I hope you see how perfectly that relates to being a Christian and sharing your faith. The "game" for Christians is the mission God has given us to make our life count here on earth. If we let our sinful nature, or even specific mistakes, distract us, then we'll end up taking ourselves out of the game.

After all that, there is one thing to remember: If you are in a continual pattern of behavior that the Bible says is wrong (drinking, uncontrolled anger, going too far sexually with your boyfriend or girlfriend, rebelling against your parents' authority, etc.) and you're not really trying to get out of it, God will likely take you out of the game until you do. He won't bring opportunities for you to help a friend because you're being a selfish player instead of an unselfish teammate.

Where is the line you have to step over before God takes you out of the game? It's in your heart. Only you and God know your real desire to follow and obey him. Consistently poor outward behavior can be a warning sign that something has malfunctioned inside; but that's *God's* call. He knows our condition, he knows how deep a destructive habit can be, and he knows whether we really want to stop. He's patient, and his patience means he still uses us as long as we're doing those four things with our mistakes.

Reflecting . . .

1 Since you know that Satan *hates* you, how do you think he responds when you blow it?

2 How does God respond?

3 Think of your last two major mistakes. Write down what you can learn from them so you don't repeat them.

Letting Your Net-Work

It was nearly Thanksgiving, and Raymond had yet to meet another Christian at his school. His family went to a medium-sized church on the other side of town, so having friends from youth group he could hang with was out. He'd met a few kids at school he could at least eat lunch with, but he definitely felt like he was all alone.

Have you heard of the word *networking*?

Gag, sounds like an adult term!

Yeah, it is. But hang with me, OK? It's a good one, so let's find out what it means.

Webster defines *networking* as "the exchange of information or services among individuals, groups, and institutions."

OK. Enough with the dictionary work.

Good News! You don't have to be a Lone Ranger trying to reach your friend for Christ. God has already placed around you "individuals, groups, and institutions" to help

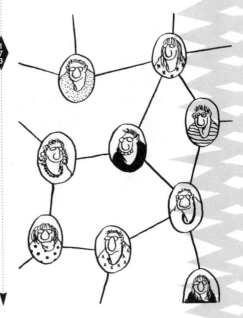

173

you hit that goal of sharing your faith.

While you may not have every one of these elements, even Raymond has two or three he can use.

Parents

Sadly, not every Christian teen comes from a Christian home. And for some who do, the parents aren't great examples or are too busy to be used by God in the life of one of your friends. Often, though—especially if you ask—Christian parents would welcome the chance to be available. How can *they* help?

- Since a lot of kids don't come from stable two-parent homes, they can serve as an example of how a family *should* be.

  Being from a divorced family situation myself, I (Greg) was always a little bit jealous of friends whose families were intact. Spending time at their houses made me feel secure. There were a couple of years during junior high that I really needed some normalcy. Hanging out at their houses provided a few hours of peace.

- If your mom and dad are cool (i.e., they don't embarrass you every time your friends are around), they can answer questions your friends have that you can't answer.

- They can pray with you about your friends. We all need that reminder and encouragement to lift our friends up to the Lord. Since he created them, he knows best how to reach them. By praying, you release God's power to work in their hearts.

Older Brothers or Sisters

It may not happen very often, but you might get lucky and actually have an older sibling who doesn't treat you like dog food. My older brother always hated my friends because most of them were smart mouths (like me). Plus, he wasn't a Christian, so why should he care two beans about them anyway? But if an older sibling is cool and doesn't mind being available to talk or answer questions, they're another source God can use to lead your friend one step closer to him.

Youth Groups, Leaders, and Sponsors

If your friend doesn't have a church background, this may or may not be the right place to bring them.

Once in a while, you'll find an adult leading a youth group who doesn't know how to relate to kids, but most of the time, they're pretty cool. They're good-hearted, they know how to keep a conversation going, they can answer questions and, hopefully, just be normal so your friend can see you don't have to be weird to be a Christian.

Sometimes, however, the group is too cliquish. If you feel your friends won't be welcomed by the group, don't bring them or they'll be immediately turned off. (And check out "How to 'De-clique' Your Youth Group" on page 159.)

Another turnoff could be the language or songs used by the leaders or kids. Church folk sometimes use unfamiliar words. It's called "Christian-ese." The sermon or the songs just don't relate to new people because they don't know the definitions of words like *redemption, incarnation,* and *born again*. Most would end up walking out at the end of the meeting not knowing what was said. (Take a quick peek at the "Stuff at the End of the Book #1" on page 199 for some common Christian jargon people outside the church don't always understand.) While *some* Christian words are helpful in starting a conversation, too many can make it confusing.

Before you invite someone to a Sunday school class or an event at your church, ask your youth leader if it will relate to someone who isn't a Christian.

Big Events

A few times a year, churches or groups do larger events designed for you to bring your non-Christian friends. There are two types: evangelistic and non-evangelistic.

Evangelistic. This type of event means someone is going to challenge those in the crowd who aren't Christians to consider becoming Christians. They may even ask them to come forward or raise their hands. Concerts, camps, and out-of-town retreats are sometimes designed to be evangelistic. Take advantage of these as often as possible, especially if your friend has heard it all and just needs a way to respond.

Important note: Make sure your friend knows what is going to happen at the camp or event. Always find out ahead of time from your leader if there will be an invitation to accept Christ. Then, when you invite your friend, you can tell them, "There's going to be a great band that plays music I know you'll love. Then one of the leaders is going to give a brief message about what it means to be a Christian. The last thing I want is for you to feel pressured, but I think you'd have a good time . . . and you might get a few of your questions answered."

By laying your cards on the table, your friend will never feel "tricked" into coming. After all, the goal is to move him one step closer to the Savior, not two steps back. Friends who are burned once will be very hesitant to come to anything church related again.

Non-evangelistic. Your church may do a game night or lock-in or even a ski trip with fun being the only goal. These events are great because your friend can see that Christians can be normal and have fun like everyone else (something many teens don't believe!). They can rub shoulders with leaders and other church friends and hopefully be attracted by what they see. Again, always find out ahead of time what type of spiritual content will be presented (if any), so you can invite your friend by giving them all the information they need to make their own choice. And if they say no, remember that it was your job to *ask* them, but it's *God's* job to get them to say yes when the time is right.

Campus Life or Young Life

On Monday nights (and other nights, of course) in cities and small towns throughout the country, these groups meet for the express purpose of building friendships with unchurched teens in order for them to hear more about Christ. Most meet in homes of students in a particular school area. The evenings are fun, sometimes wacky, and very low-key. The leader will begin a discussion on a topic your friends can relate to and will usually give a brief talk to wrap up the evening. This can be a

great place to take friends. Other Christian groups you may find in your area are Student Venture and Fellowship of Christian Athletes.

If the group is unfamiliar to you, check it out for about four weeks first and get the feel of it (one or two weeks won't tell you anything). If you feel welcomed and the night is fun for you, your friend may feel the same. A good idea is to ask one of the leaders for an appointment after school sometime. Get to know them and find out where the group is going. Let them share their vision.

Be aware that these groups are not like a church youth group. The spiritual content of the message will likely not be as strong, and there may not even be any singing! While the goal is to lead teens to Christ, long-term friendships are the key to accomplishing that goal. Spiritual information is given, but it comes in bite-sized chunks. This method of "relational evangelism" is very effective. The students and leaders who are using it as a tool to reach teens know the value of "winning the right to be heard" before crossing the bridge with the gospel. Often, the group will point toward a future camp or retreat where it's easier to talk one-on-one with those who are considering becoming Christians.

If your youth group doesn't have "entry-level" meetings or events where a friend can ease into Christian stuff, then these can be a great option.

Christian Teachers

Though Christian teachers have to be very careful about what they do during school hours, there are thousands who are making an incredible impact on students at their school. Their example, wisdom, concern, and availability put them in a unique position.

If you want to start a Bible study before or after school, you must have a teacher commit to supervising it. (In most school districts they can't lead it.)

Find out who the Christian teachers are at your school, and tap into their influence and position of authority to help reach others.

Reflecting . . .

1 What specific spiritual activities have helped strengthen *your* walk with God?

2 What are the options at your church or school group where you could take your non-Christian friends to:
a. have fun?
b. hear the gospel?

Choose Your Own Break

Time for a breather! Stand up, put the book down,
pretend you're someone famous, and do one of the following:

1. Fold a banana

2. Count the bumps in your bedroom ceiling

3. Shake hands with yourself

4. Stick your little bro's toothbrush in the dishwasher (probably couldn't *hurt*)

5. Use neon paint to put your address on the curb outside your home (better check with Mom or Dad first in case they are allergic to paint smells, are embarrassed to let people know where you live, wanna do it themselves, or don't have a curb)

6. Create a new cover for your least-fave textbook

7. Mark Susie's B-day in your calendar (September 12)

8. Mark Greg's B-day in your calendar (July 11)

9. Change *your* birthday, and mark it in your calendar

10. Gargle with peanut butter

Treating Aliens like Real People

Dear Greg:

I have this friend who was an atheist, claims to be Buddhist, and also says he was a Christian at one time. He has some very interesting theories, like aliens created the world. My other friend and I keep talking to him about the one, true God, but he just laughs.

Once I took him to a Teens for Christ lock-in. We heard an awesome testimony. When it was all over, he just said he can become a Christian or anything else whenever he wants. Do you have any ideas on how to help him? Besides, that is, making him feel stupid, screaming at him at the top of my lungs, or preaching uncontrollably?

ST. CHARLES, MISSOURI

It sounds like *he's* the alien! And there's one thing about aliens: they sure are different!

While it seems like your friend

is enjoying pushing your buttons, let's pretend he's on the level—that he really does have . . . "different" beliefs.

Some people aren't comfortable putting their beliefs in a neat little package. OK, that's good. But at the

179

same time he's not really not sure *what* he believes. Actually, it sounds like he may be a real seeker looking for the truth. While he's never seen an alien and likely doesn't know what a Buddhist is, it's safe to assume he's *not* a Christian.

Getting through to people with the truth about Jesus doesn't ever need to get out of hand. While it may be frustrating to hear someone else talk about aliens like he knows they exist, let him talk. True seekers won't stick to illogical beliefs long if they're really looking for the truth. Those who aren't really seeking won't stick to them either . . . if they don't get any attention!

Stay cool, and instead of trying to convince him of anything, give your opinion when asked. Yes, you may feel an urgency because you know that bad beliefs combined with a drunk driver could put your friend in hell tomorrow, but you can't argue someone into the kingdom—ever.

Here are a few tips:

- Try to live your life as consistently as you can so he can see what a real Christian looks like. While it's always tough to have it all together, do your best. (We've hit on this a couple of times . . . has it stuck yet?)
- Answer his questions or his outrageous remarks according to his seriousness. If he's joking or trying to set you off, laugh with him. If you're not sure whether he's serious, ask him. If he is, reply in a calm manner.
- Give him time and space. Work on being a great all-around friend. Talk about other things besides where he's going to spend eternity. Stick with him—if he'll let you. He'll either head off the deep end and dump you, or he'll edge closer to the truth.

He sounds like the type who may come to Christ after a long search. These people have gone through so many lies, they'll usually be *very* committed to the truth once they find it.

In my opinion, he's worth your investment. It could pay big dividends later on.

So What It All Comes Down To...

You care about your friends. You really want them to know Christ as their personal Savior, or you wouldn't have read this far. And now you know how to give your testimony, how to help hurting friends, how to encourage others to make a spiritual commitment . . . but now what?

NOW IT'S TIME! With your help, your friend has come to the realization that he needs God. He knows his life will eventually end in despair if he doesn't make a spiritual decision. Now's the time to lead him in a prayer of faith that will change his life!

He's ready. This is the moment you've prepared for and prayed for. You're jazzed. Before we pray, let's go over a few basics with him first, OK? Let's call him Matt. ▼

You might want to say something like this:

"Matt, I'm excited that you've decided to follow God. Is it OK if I just run through a couple of reminders first before we pray together?"

"Yeah, sure."

Reminder #1

"You realize you can't make it to heaven on your own; you need God's help. In fact, we need God's help just to make it through *life*, right?"

"Gotcha."

"OK, but here's the catch: God *loves* you and *wants* you in heaven, but since he can't allow sin into his kingdom you're eternally separated from him . . . because you (like all of us) were *born* with sin."

"Yeah, and I'm tired of the sin in my life."

"Good. We're moving now. And you know that God not only has the power to forgive your sins, but he also wants to forgive your sins."

"Yeah, I believe that. And I also believe that Jesus died for my sins."

"That's exactly right, Matt. He loved you *so much* he gave his very *life* for you! That's pretty exciting. In fact, if you were the only one in the whole world, he still would have died just for you."

"Blows my mind."

"Mine, too. And you know that all you have to do to be forgiven of your sins is to ask God, right?"

"Yep. I got it. It's a free gift. I can't earn it, can't buy it, don't deserve it, but know I *want* it, so let's pray."

"OK, OK. Just one more reminder."

Reminder #2

"You might *feel* something; you might not. I mean, some people say they felt like the earth moved or something when they gave their life to Christ. Others don't feel *anything*. Remember, you're not basing your walk with God on *feeling*, you're grounding it in *faith*."

"Will I *ever* feel God?"

"Yeah, probably, but I don't know *for sure*. I think it's somewhat different for each person. But, hey, if you *don't* feel him, does that mean you're not gonna believe he's in your heart?"

"I hope not. I mean, I wanna believe."

"Good. Because you don't always feel the sun, do you?"

"No."

"You can't always feel it, and sometimes you can't even *see* it, but you know it's still there, right?"

"Sure."

"Works the same way in your relationship with Christ. You may not *see* or *feel* him, but you'll learn to recognize his voice, and you'll talk with him and he'll guide you. I mean, he becomes your very Best Friend."

"Yeah! That's what I want . . . someone I can always depend on."

"Well, God is certainly dependable. He's promised he'll never *ever* leave us. But, Matt, he wants to be much more than your Best Friend.

He also wants to be Lord of your life. Are you ready to give him *everything?*"

"Yeah. I am."

"Great! Let's pray."

"I don't really know what to say."

"Tell you what; I'll pray and you just repeat the words after me."

"Yeah, I like that."

Father, thanks for loving me so much that you sent your Son to die for me. I don't understand why, and I don't really deserve it, but thanks! I'm sorry for the sin in my life.

I confess that I need you and am asking your forgiveness. From now on I want to live for you. I'm tired of running my own life and calling my own shots. I want you to be in charge.

Come into my life and take over. Make me a brand-new person. I give you everything I am and everything I hope to be. I'm asking you to remake me and mold me in your image.

I know I can't live a godly life on my own, so I ask that you would fill me with the power of your Holy Spirit. I realize that you give me power that makes a godly life possible.

I believe your Word is the absolute truth, Jesus. And because you promised to forgive our sins when we asked, I believe that you have done that just now for me.

Thank you, Father, for living in my life now; for owning me. Thanks for making me brand-new. I love you, Jesus. Amen.

"Matt, the Bible tells us that when even *one person* accepts Christ as his personal Savior that all of heaven rejoices."

"They're partying big-time, huh?"

"They sure are! You've just made the most important decision of your life. But one more thing I gotta remind you of before we go grab a Coke . . . and that's the fact that you have some spiritual responsibilities now."

"Whaddya mean?"

"Christ lives in your heart now, but his Word tells us to *walk in the light as he is in the light* (it's all through the second chapter of 1 John). In other words, it's your responsibility to *grow!*"

"How do I *do* that?"

"Read your Bible and pray. Spend time with God *daily*. Take your relationship with him seriously. Keep it as the most important thing in your life."

"I will."

"This wasn't just some magic, flippant prayer you shot up to heaven. This is just the beginning. Grow and cultivate your faith just like a plant. Nurture it, protect it, deepen your roots, and take *good* care of it."

"Yeah! Now let's go grab a couple of Cokes and tell Jamie!"

"Now That I've Learned to Walk, Where Do I Go?"

Dear Susie:

One of my friends just gave her life to Christ at a concert our youth group attended. I want to make sure she sticks with it. She doesn't have a Christian family. How can I help her?

WICHITA, KANSAS

She *can* have a Christian family. Your church can be her family! I'm excited that your friend's name is now written in the Book of Life . . . and I'm also jazzed that you care enough about her to help her grow spiritually.

Many times when we see someone commit their life to the Lord, we think, *Whew, I'm glad they're a Christian now. I'll start looking for someone else I can witness to.*

Just because a baby takes a few steps doesn't mean he's learned to

walk, does it? He still falls down a lot. But if he has loving parents, they'll pick him up and hold his hand and walk *with* him, until he's mastered the skill and can walk alone.

Works kind of the same way

AAAH! I'M NOT PERFECT ENOUGH TO WITNESS!

185

spiritually. Your friend has just made the most important decision in her life! But it's still all new to her. There's a lot she doesn't understand. How can she grow? How can she learn to walk on her own?

Don't Put the Baby Down till He's Burped

Just because a baby has consumed a jar of gunky baby food doesn't mean he's finished eating. If he doesn't burp, he'll get sick. (You would too, if you ate that stuff!) The wise parent knows they need to rock, hold, and gently pat the baby on his back until he burps.

Well, you're kind of a "spiritual parent" to your friend. You've fed her some terrific spiritual food. But you're not finished with her yet. Gently "hold" her till she burps. (Not *literally*, of course! But stick with me. I promise it'll all make sense in a sec.)

Help her digest all the spiritual food that's inside her. There's a lot she doesn't understand. Be willing to explain and answer questions. You probably won't know it all. That's OK. Take her to your youth leader or other adults in your life who can help.

Or you could buy her a great book Greg wrote. It's called *If I Could Ask God One Question* . . . It has sixty-five answers to questions new and young Christians ask.

Candy Bars and Coke . . . or Meat and Veggies?

It's good to involve your new Christian friend in youth group parties, ski trips, and pizza flings. She needs to know that Christ is her very best friend. You can help her learn that he laughs with her, hurts with her, and *understands* her.

But that's kind of like just eating candy bars and drinking Cokes. They sure taste good! And it *feels* good to consume 'em. But to be healthy, we need more than just sugar in our diet. We need meat and veggies, too, don't we? Yeah, I know, they're not as much fun and don't taste as good . . . but if we don't get what we need we won't grow properly.

Works the same way *spiritually*. Church parties and ski trips and pizza flings are a blast! But there has to be more. If your new Christian friend is really going to g-r-o-w spiritually, she needs some meat and veggies: some Bible study, worship experience, and accountability.

So while helping her learn that Christianity is a blast, don't forget to involve her in other aspects of spiritual growth that are also important. Plug her into a church (possibly yours), a Sunday school class (to provide accountability . . . that means someone asks where she is when she misses), and a Bible study to help her deepen her spiritual roots.

Don't Throw the Baby Out with the Bathwater!

She's still a baby Christian. So it's understandable she'll fail. That's OK. That doesn't mean she's "lost" it or just can't cut being a Christian. It's *normal* to make mistakes. Remember when you first learned to ride a bicycle? You fell, scraped your knees, maybe even ran into your neighbor's mailbox—but you didn't quit. You kept on until you got the hang of it.

Please don't give up on your friend when she blows it. Encourage her. Remind her to ask for God's forgiveness, accept it, then get up and keep walking.

There may be some habits in her life that she needs to get rid of. It's not *your* job to point out all the bad

stuff you see. That's *God's* job. You're not his "sin monitor." Let *him* deal with it in *his* perfect timing.

But as she begins to wrestle with some of these issues (possibly drinking, smoking, cussing, her sex life), you can help her learn to see and understand what God wants and expects. When she asks you (yes, wait until you're asked, don't *tell*) if you think she should go out with Mark (who's a heavy drinker), you can share that as a new Christian it might be too big a temptation for her.

Then if she goes out anyway and drinks and tells you about it later, don't throw out the baby with the bathwater. I understand you'll be frustrated. You want her to "hurry and grow up" spiritually. But growth takes time, doesn't it?

Offer to pray with her. Seek God's forgiveness, then "toss out"

Reflecting . . .

1 Name three people you can "connect" your new Christian friend with so they won't depend solely on you.

2 What are the most important things new Christians need to learn? What are the best ways to teach them?

the habit of going out with those who will tempt (just like you'd "toss out" old bathwater), and continue walking forward.

MOST IMPORTANT: Let your friend know you care about her spiritual growth. Don't abandon her. Stick close and introduce her to *more* Christian friends she can hang out with.

188

The Unknown Influencer

Before you read our last incredible chapter, we want to let you know that we're not stupid. We know stepping out and sharing your faith isn't as easy as breathing. There are a ton of fears you have to deal with, and maybe even a few unanswered questions that leave you unconvinced. Some of these fears and questions we've mentioned, some we haven't. Here's the short list of reasons you might not be sharing your faith:

- You have a fear of the unknown.
- You're afraid of being rejected by friends who may exclude you from the group if you act "too religious."
- You're not really convinced that people are actually drowning in their sin.

- You don't think God has gifted you to share your faith.
- You don't know what to say.
- You think your hormones are too active, and that you're too imperfect to be a consistent example.

- No one has ever showed you how.
- You don't have any friends who aren't already Christians.
- You still don't know how to start a conversation with someone who has a different value system than yours.
- You don't think you know enough about the Bible to answer a friend's questions.
- You're afraid of offending someone.
- You think only "professionals" should share their faith.
- You're tired of feeling guilty for what you're not doing and have given up.
- At this stage of your Christian life, you have enough troubles of your own, and you just don't have time to care that much about other people's problems.

You're Not Alone

Every Christian who has finally taken the risk to be the "ultimate best friend" has used one or more of those "excuses" before they moved beyond their fear and dove in.

If you decide to stick with Christ, you'll eventually realize that he saved you FROM something FOR something.

A friend of mine once asked me what was keeping me (Greg) from climbing the largest peak in the Northwest, Mount Rainier. The ex-

cuses came easy, and I was sure I'd convinced him I'd never attempt it.

- It was too risky.
- I wasn't properly trained.
- I didn't have the right equipment.
- I wasn't in shape.

He looked at me and said, "I can help you overcome every one of those reasons, but it still wouldn't be enough to convince you that you could really do it."

I smiled and said, "You're right. The real problem is in my mind."

He laughed and said, "That's right."

He knew I really didn't *want* to climb Mount Rainier. I didn't think it was important enough to even try getting prepared for.

He Gave It All

Stephen was a man who was probably just like you and me . . . until he heard about Jesus and became a Christian. Then he grew steadily in his faith, and one day he had the chance to share all he knew with hundreds of people who didn't believe in Jesus. He gave one of the most powerful, logical sermons recorded in the Bible. His words, though filled with truth, fell on ears that didn't want to hear. He knew it, too, but it didn't change his mind about what he knew he had to do.

As he was finishing, the people

who were listening were so ticked off they picked up rocks (larger than a hand, smaller than a head) and threw them at him until he uttered these last words: "Lord, do not hold this sin against them." Then he died. (See Acts 7 for the full story.)

There was no "invitation" and no record that day of anyone who became a Christian because of Stephen's words. But there was *one* man in the crowd who heard every word. He even held all his buddies' coats while they threw the rocks that killed Stephen (he must have had a bad arm that week). His name was Saul.

A few days later, Saul was so angry at those who believed in Christ that he got permission to go to a faraway town to have them arrested and brought back for trial and, hopefully, execution.

Though the Bible doesn't say exactly what Saul was thinking about as he traveled in the hot sun that day, he may have been replaying the death of Stephen over and over in his mind. Suddenly, Jesus Christ appeared to him and told him what he must do to be saved (Acts 9:1-31).

This Saul later took the Latin name of Paul. He traveled the whole known world sharing his faith and planting churches. He wound up writing all of the New Testament books between Romans and Philemon. After Paul recognized the

truth about Jesus Christ, I'm sure he remembered the faith of one obedient Christian who stood for the truth—Stephen. A man who would never live to see the fruit of his labors, but who risked it all for his faith in Christ.

It's Happening All the Time

As I said earlier, I wasn't a Christian in high school. Yet I watched those who said they were. There were a few in particular I wished I could have been like, but I didn't understand what they had. One guy named Jim, class valedictorian and a grade-school friend of mine, spoke at our graduation. His talk was on 1 Corinthians 13. I don't remember a thing he said. But I remember going up to him afterwards with tears in my eyes and saying, "I was going to wish you good luck, but I can tell that you don't need luck. You have something else." After I became a Christian, he was the first guy I told.

I can't understand, nor can I believe, all that God has done with my life since that day I became one of his kids. Jim wasn't the ONLY reason I became a Christian, but God used him—and others—to point me in the direction of real LIFE.

People are watching your life even now. No, they're probably not thinking what a neat person you are, and how much they want to be like you (younger teens, especially, aren't that smart). They're simply noticing how you treat them, how you treat others, and how you live your life. You may not ever get the chance to share your faith with them, but one day, they'll remember the person who was "different"—in a good sort of way. And who knows what they will go on to do or become?

Be that *quiet* influence.

Be that *vocal* influence, too, if you have the courage, and if it's appropriate. Realize, too, that it's not just your friends' eternity that's at stake; it's all those people *they* could influence in the years to come because of you.

Reflecting . . .

1 What are some common excuses people give for not telling others about their faith in God?

2 What's your most common excuse?

3 Who are the people in your life who have influenced you toward Christ but perhaps don't know it?

4 What did they do that made such an impact?

5 Write down three people you know who may be watching your life today.

Will You Be the One?

Long before Al Denson began singing "Will You Be the One?" God was asking the question. Throughout the course of time he has used ordinary people to impact their world. *Ordinary* people. People with only one or two talents. People like you and me, who sometimes get angry and lonely and hate practicing the piano.

And through *ordinary, everyday people,* God defeated armies, turned a small group of slaves into a great nation, split seas, healed the sick, and melted the hardened hearts of sinners.

All this and more through people like you and me . . . who were *willing to be used.* THAT'S the key. Are *you* willing? Would *you* dare to *be the one?*

Daniel dared. Moses dared. Abraham dared. So did Noah, Enoch,

Abel, Sarah, Jacob, and Joseph. Jonah? Well, . . . *he* was a different story. And if *you're* trying to decide whether or not to "be the one" to share your faith, maybe you oughta take a quick peek at Jonah's situation.

LET'S REVIEW
1. GIVE YOUR LIFE TO CHRIST.
2. ASK GOD TO FORGIVE YOUR SINS.
3. PRAY.

Let's set the scene.

Place: Nineveh. Old city. Population: approximately 120,000 with more people constantly moving in. Fastest-growing city of its time.

Problem: City with a bad rep. Quickly becoming more and more wicked. (You've heard of other wicked places in the Bible: Sodom, Gomorrah, and the whole world in Noah's time!)

Solution: Destroy the city. *Hmmm.* Has to be a better plan. Sure would be a tragedy for 120,000 people to die without ever knowing they *could* have received forgiveness for their sins and lived a better life.

Better Solution: Have someone tell them about God.

Newly Recruited Be-the-One Spokesman: Jonah

Complication: Jonah didn't *wanna* "be the one." Too selfish. Too lazy. Too comfortable watching TV.

Further Complication: God *commanded* him to "be the one." (*Repeat after me:* When God speaks, it makes sense to obey.)

What Happened: Jonah was a whiner. He complained that Nineveh was too far. Also a little too wild. Yep, he'd heard of their bad rep and didn't want to spoil his *good* rep by hanging around those people. Jonah *wanted* God to destroy them! Thought they deserved it. (*Hmmm.*

Sounds like he needed an attitude check, huh?)

So he went to a travel agent and bought a ticket for a cruise, thinking if he ran far enough away, sooner or later God would just forget the whole thing.

This was no "Love Boat." The *Pacific Princess* he set sail on was full of superstitious sailors. Instead of trying to share his faith with them, he went to the bottom of the ship to catch some Zs. (All that running from God had worn him out!)

But God knew *exactly* where Jonah was. (He always knows where *we* are, too.) And he allowed a terrible storm to erupt at sea. It was such a nightmare that even those rough, macho sailors (who were *professional* seamen) were frightened!

They knew Jonah was a religious man. (They saw him wearing his "See You at the Pole" ID bracelet and noticed his Bible stacked with his luggage.) So they woke him up and begged him to pray for their safety.

Pray for *them?* Jonah didn't feel like praying for *anyone!* His conscience bothered him too much. The ship continued to weave back and forth, back and forth, back and . . . (Are you getting seasick yet?). Fifteen-foot waves emptied themselves on board. Mighty scary times.

Even though Jonah was acting like a jerk, he still had one thing going for him. *He was honest.* So he straightened his back and fessed up. "I'm the reason for this storm," he volunteered.

Guess what the sailors did? They tossed him overboard!

But God wasn't finished with our be-the-one recruit just yet. (You already know this part of the story because you've heard it since you were in kindergarten.) The Lord sent a huge fish ('bout the size of a mammoth whale, which is probably the size of a football field . . . well, *maybe*) to swallow Jonah.

Gross, huh? Jonah spent three days and three nights in his new home. Lots of fish 'n' chips for dinner! Talk about BORING. *What can you do in the belly of a whale?* (1) Untangle the intestines, then measure them; (2) backstroke through the stomach juices; (3) taste the gastric acids; (4) chip off the ol' bone marrow; (5) make seaweed soup for breakfast; (6) alphabetize all the stuff a whale eats—like license plates, people, shoes, octopi, school buses; (7) think.

Jonah chose the last one. He thought. And thought. And thought some more. I think he realized his back was against a wall. Listen to what he says in Jonah 2:7: "When I had lost all hope, I turned my thoughts once more to the Lord" (TLB).

Typical, huh? When we've lost ▼

all hope, THEN we turn to the Lord! Things *could* have been *so much better* if he'd just obeyed in the first place! But he tried to do things his own way and ended up inside the digestive system of a giant fish!

Gag! (Literally.) God caused the fish to gag, and Jonah came out in its vomit. You're right, it's gross. Makes much more sense to obey God's commands the first time around.

Jonah went straight to Nineveh and began preaching. He told the people if they didn't turn from their wicked ways, the Lord would destroy their city in forty days.

He still needed an attitude check, though, because when the people got interested enough to stop and listen, Jonah secretly wished they'd continue on their merry way and die in sin.

But the people were intrigued! They never realized there was an all-powerful God who cared about how they lived! (Your friends will be intrigued too, when you begin sharing *your* faith.) They prayed, asked God to forgive their sins, turned from their wicked ways, and cleaned up their act.

The *king* even gave his life to God, then ordered everyone else to do the same! (Wow. *That's* throwing your power around, huh?)

Jonah took his lousy attitude and waited underneath a shade tree outside the city gates, hoping, wishing, and pleading for God to burn the city down with fire from heaven. But God didn't. He didn't need to, now. The mission had been successful. The citizens of Nineveh were now Christians! (Well, *believers,* anyway.)

So what did Jonah do? Praise God for using him? Nope. He threw a temper tantrum!

This is exactly what I thought you'd do, Lord, when I was there in my own country and you first told me to come here. That's why I ran away to Tarshish. For I knew you were a gracious God, merciful, slow to get angry, and full of kindness; I knew how easily you could cancel your plans for destroying these people. Please kill me, Lord. I'd rather be dead than alive [when nothing that I told them happens]. (Jonah 4:2-3, TLB)

Wowsers. Attitude check, Jonah. Why are you so concerned about what people are going to think of *you,* rather than being excited that God used you to make a difference in thousands of lives?

Then the Lord said, "Is it right to be angry about this?" (Jonah 4:4, TLB)

Jonah just continued to sit . . . outside . . . in the sun . . . underneath a shade tree . . . and *sulked!* ▼

Then a worm started chewing on the shade tree, and it withered. So Jonah began complaining about *that!* (Some people never learn, huh?)

Without the shade tree, he got a severe sunburn and was so miserable and physically sick he pleaded with God to let him die!

"Death is better than this!"

And God said to Jonah, "Is it right for you to be angry because the plant died?"

"Yes," Jonah said, "it is; it is right for me to be angry enough to die!" (Jonah 4:8-9, TLB)

Maybe God should have granted his wish right then, but he probably didn't want Jonah hanging around in heaven with that kind of an attitude, so he continued to deal with him. There was still an important lesson for Jonah to learn. God wasn't finished with him yet!

Then the Lord said, "You feel sorry for yourself when your shelter is destroyed, though you did no work to put it there. . . . Why shouldn't I feel sorry for a great city like Nineveh with its 120,000 people in utter spiritual darkness?" (Jonah 4:10-11, TLB)

Wow. Kind of hits you between the eyes, doesn't it? (God has a way of doing that sometimes.) People in your school are in utter spiritual darkness! Yet we get so caught up in our own little world that all we can think of is complaining about petty, unimportant things.

Your friends are dying! What could be more important than sharing God with them? What could possibly be as high a priority as "being the one"?

I like Isaiah's attitude. Check *this* out:

> Then I heard the Lord asking, "Whom shall I send as a messenger to my people? Who will go?"
> And I said, "Lord, I'll go! Send me." (Isaiah 6:8, TLB)

Will *you* go?

Decision time:

A. Yes, I want to impact others

for you, Lord. I *care* that my friends are going to hell! Use *me* to make a difference.

B. Too much trouble. I'm too scared. It's their own fault.

Hint: The rewards for choosing A are beyond your imagination!

So . . . *will you be the one?*

"Be the One"

In a world full of broken dreams
Where the truth is hard to find
For every promise that is kept
There are many left behind
Though it seems that nobody cares
It still matters what you do
'Cause there's a difference you can make
But the choice is up to you

197

Reflecting . . .

1 What does Matthew 5:13-14 have to say about "being the one"?

2 Can you identify a specific time in *your* life when you ran from doing what God wanted you to do? How did you feel? Looking back, would it have been easier to have obeyed him in the first place?

3 If *you* don't tell your friends about the Lord, who will?

Will you be the one
To answer to his call
Will you stand
When those around you fall
Will you be the one
To take his light
Into a darkened world
Tell me will you be the one

Oh sometimes it's hard to know
Who is right and what is wrong
And where are you supposed to
    stand
When the battle lines are drawn
There's a voice that is calling out
For someone who's not afraid
To be a beacon in the night

To a world that's lost its way
There are still some battles
That I must fight from day to day
Yet the Lord provides the power
For me to stand and say

I will be the one
To answer to his call
I will stand
When those around me fall
I will be the one
To take his light
Into a darkened world
I will be the one.

Do You Speak "Christianese"?

Your friends who aren't Christians probably don't. One way to show you care about someone is to speak a language they can understand. If you absolutely have to say the words on the left, explain them. On the right you'll see a brief explanation. One rule to live by: Don't use words you can't explain.

Accept Jesus/Never mentioned in the Bible. Closest reference is John 1:12. Means to *take* the free *gift* of forgiveness, to believe Jesus paid the penalty for your sin nature, and to choose to become one of God's kids.

Into your heart/No one asks a bearded, Jewish Messiah to take up residence in his aorta. Accepting Jesus *into your heart* means asking him to guide your will. God's Spirit,

however, does actually enter a person who is humble enough to admit his need for a Savior.

Sin/In the Middle Ages, when archers missed a target, the spotter would say, "Sin." If they hit it, they would say, "Mark." *Sin* means to "miss the mark." Romans 3:23 is clear—all have sinned.

Personal Savior/Again, not mentioned in the Bible. It's a shorter way to say that God treats everyone as individuals—he's personal. And everyone needs to choose whether they want Jesus to pay for their ticket to heaven—as their Savior. An alternative choice is to take their chances on finding another way. (Please note: There isn't another way. See John 14:6.)

199

Confess/In Bible verses such as Romans 10:9, *confess* does *not* mean to admit you're wrong. It simply means to openly state something with your mouth, to say, "Well, everybody, here's what I believe."

Repent/Literally means that if you're heading one direction (away from God), you turn around and head the other way (toward him). No matter how many steps someone walks away from God, when he turns around, God is right there next to him (1 John 1:9). True repentance occurs when the heart has changed (Romans 10:9).

Born again/A word picture Jesus used once with a man named Nicodemus (see John 3:3). It means to start all over again as a newborn in God's family. Your first birth you don't remember (ask your mom—she does!). The second birth—a spiritual birth—occurs when you decide to allow God to forgive your sin and make yourself available to be led by his Holy Spirit.

Redeem/redemption/Trading something in to get something back. Example: Jesus gave his life on the cross so man could once again have a great relationship with God (like in the Garden of Eden). Pretty phenomenal!

Salvation/saved/It's what happens when we say, "God, I want Jesus to pay the penalty for my sin nature." We become saved from an eternity away from God (or, to get real specific, hell!).

Scripture/The Bible. Everything God thought was important for us to know, he put there. Though he's silent on many things (dinosaurs, fusion, etc.), he's not silent about showing his deep love for people.

Righteousness/Having a right relationship with God. We either get right with God, or get left . . . left out of the party when he returns.

Fellowship with God/Having confidence that you can *really* communicate with the Creator of EVERYTHING! By realizing *and* acting on the fact that God wants to spend time with humans, you have fellowship with him.

Your Most Important Relationship

If you've wondered how to explain the most important facts about your faith to someone else, the following is a great tool to use with your friends. It comes in a booklet format and can be ordered in any quantity you'd like.

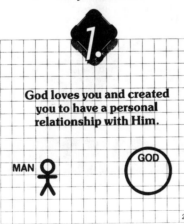

YOU were created with value and worth.
God wants your life to count.

Did you know . . .

1.

God loves you and created you to have a personal relationship with Him.

MAN

GOD

2

God created you.
In Psalm 139:13-14 the Bible says, "You made all the delicate, inner parts of my body, and knit them together in my mother's womb. Thank you for making me so wonderfully complex!"

God loves you.
"For God loved the world so much that he gave his only Son so that anyone who believes in him shall not perish but have eternal life." (John 3:16)

God wants you to know him.
"And this is the way to have eternal life — by knowing you, the only true God, and Jesus Christ, the one you sent to earth!" (John 17:3)

3

Why is it that many people do not have a personal relationship with God?

2.

Our sin keeps us from having a personal relationship with God.

MAN   GOD

SIN

4

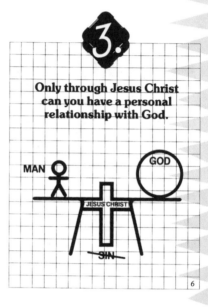

3.

Only through Jesus Christ can you have a personal relationship with God.

MAN   GOD

JESUS CHRIST

SIN

6

2 0 2

What is sin?

"Knowing what is right to do and then not doing it is sin." (James 4:17) You see, God is holy and perfect . . . and we are not. Sin not only means doing wrong or failing to do all that God wants. Sin is also our attitude of ignoring or rejecting God. Because God is holy, he cannot accept our sin.

Who has sinned?

"Yes, they all have sinned; all fall short of God's glorious ideal ; . . ." (Romans 3:23)

What happens when we sin?

"But the trouble is that your sins have cut you off from God." (Isaiah 59:2) "For the wages of sin is death." (Romans 6:23) Sin causes a gap between God and us. Death, which means eternal separation from God, is the penalty of our sin.

5

What is the solution to our separation from God?

Why Jesus Christ?

In John 14:6 Jesus said, "I am the Way – yes, and the Truth and the Life. No one can get to the Father except by means of me." It is only through Jesus Christ that we can have a relationship with God.

Why did Jesus Christ have to die?

"He died once for the sins of all us guilty sinners, although he himself was innocent of any sin at any time, that he might bring us safely home to God." (1 Peter 3:18) Jesus died to pay the penalty for our sins, so we might be forgiven.

Why did Christ rise from the dead?

Jesus Christ rose from the dead to prove he could give us eternal life. "Christ died for our sins just as the Scriptures said he would . . . he was buried . . . three days afterwards he arose from the grave just as the prophets foretold . . . he was seen by more than five hundred Christian brothers at one time . . ." (1 Corinthians 15:3-6)

7

How can you begin your personal relationship with God?

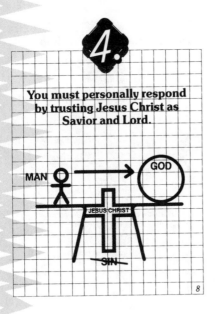

You must personally respond by trusting Jesus Christ as Savior and Lord.

MAN · GOD · JESUS CHRIST · SIN

8

203

Where would you place yourself in this illustration?

☐ I don't have a personal relationship. ☐ I would like a personal relationship. ☐ I have a personal relationship.

MAN · GOD · JESUS CHRIST · SIN

10

Where would you like to be?

You respond with trust in Christ.

In Ephesians 2:8-9 the Bible says, "Because of his kindness you have been saved through trusting Christ. And even trusting is not of yourselves; it too is a gift from God. Salvation is not a reward for the good we have done, so none of us can take any credit for it."

You respond by turning to God from sin.

"Now change your mind and attitude to God and turn to him so he can cleanse away your sins . . . ." (Acts 3:19)

You respond by receiving Christ.

"To all who received him, he gave the right to become children of God. All they needed to do was to trust him to save them." (John 1:12)

Receiving Christ means:

- **Turning** to God from your own way of living (repentance).
- **Inviting** Christ to come into your life and trusting him to forgive your sin.
- **Allowing** God to direct your life.

Receiving Jesus Christ is not just an emotional experience; nor is it just agreeing with your mind that Jesus is the Son of God. It means *total trust,* an act of your will.

9

You can begin your personal relationship with God by receiving Jesus Christ by faith.

You can express your faith (trust) through prayer. Prayer is simply talking to God. He knows what you mean even when it is difficult to express yourself. You may use the following words or your own.

"Dear God, I know that my sin has separated me from you. Thank you that Jesus Christ died in my place. I ask Jesus to forgive my sin and to come into my life. Please begin to direct my life. Thank you for giving me eternal life. In Jesus' name, Amen."

Can you say this to God, and mean it?

If you can, pray right now and trust Jesus to forgive your sin and come into your life, as he promised.

11

What's next?

5.

Your trust in Jesus Christ begins a lifelong relationship.

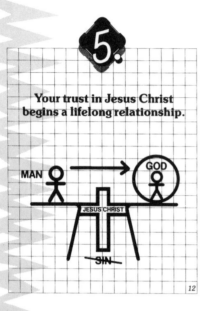

12

Do not depend upon feelings.

No matter how you feel, God always remains committed to you. The promises in God's Word, the Bible, are your authority. This illustration shows the relationship between **fact** (God and his Word), **faith** (our trust in God and his Word) and our **feelings**.

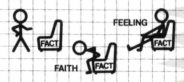

Your **faith** in the **fact** that a chair will support you causes you to act by sitting in the chair. The result is that you **feel** the comfort of the chair's strength. Even when you don't feel relaxed in the chair, it continues to support you. In the same way, you must rely on the factual promises of God's Word, rather than your feelings. Good feelings may come and go, but the **fact** of God's love for you and his forgiveness remain consistent.

14

God commits himself to you.

- God assures you that Jesus Christ has come into your life. In John 14:20 Jesus says, ". . . I am in **my Father, and you in me, and I in you.**"
- God will never leave you. "**I will never, *never* fail you nor forsake you.**" (Hebrews 13:5)
- God completely forgives your sin. "**For he forgave all your sins, and blotted out the charges proved against you.**" (Colossians 2:13-14)
- God assures you that you have eternal life. "**I have written this to you who believe in the Son of God so you may know that you have eternal life.**" (1 John 5:13)
- God gives you his Holy Spirit to enable you to live the Christian life. "**Let us follow the Holy Spirit's leading in every part of our lives.**" (Galatians 5:25)

Wouldn't you like to stop and thank God that Christ is in your life and will never leave you?

You commit yourself to God.

In Colossians 2:6-7 the Bible says, "**And now just as you trusted Christ to save you, trust him, too, for each day's problems ; . . See that you go on growing in the Lord, and become strong and vigorous . . . .**"

13

To keep growing in your relationship with God . . .

Go to God daily in prayer.
Philippians 4:6-7

Read the Bible every day.
2 Timothy 3:14-17

Obey God moment by moment.
Luke 6:46-48

Worship in a local church regularly.
Hebrews 10:24-25

Tell others about Jesus Christ.
1 Peter 3:15-16

Holy Spirit – let him direct your life.
John 14:26

Now you can share your most important relationship.

"**It is God himself who has made us what we are and given us new lives from Christ Jesus; and long ages ago he planned that we should spend these lives in helping others.**" (Ephesians 2:10) Share this booklet with a friend.

15

For copies of this in booklet form, write: YFC Sales, P.O. Box 228822, Denver, CO 80222, or call (303) 843-9000. They sell for 15 cents each.

Old Testament Prophecies Fulfilled by Jesus

		O.T. Prophecy	N.T. Fulfillment
1	Messiah to be born in Bethlehem	Micah 5:2	Matthew 2:1-6 Luke 2:1-20
2	Messiah was to be born of a virgin	Isaiah 7:14	Matthew 1:18-25 Luke 1:26-36
3	Messiah would teach in parables	Psalm 78:2	Matthew 13:34
4	Messiah was to enter Jerusalem on a donkey	Zechariah 9:9	Matthew 21:1-9 John 12:12-16
5	Messiah was to be rejected by his own people	Isaiah 53:1, 3 Psalm 118:22	Matthew 26:3-4 John 12:37-43
6	Messiah was to be betrayed by a follower	Psalm 41:9	Matthew 26:14-16, 47-50 Luke 22:19-23
7	Betrayed for thirty pieces of silver	Zechariah 11:13	Matthew 26:15; 27:3-7
8	Messiah was to be tried and condemned	Isaiah 53:8	Luke 23:1-25 Matthew 27:1-2

		O.T. Prophecy	N.T. Fulfillment
9	Messiah was to be silent before his accusers	Isaiah 53:7	Matthew 27:12-14 Mark 15:3-5 Luke 23:8-10
10	Messiah was to be smitten and spat upon by enemies	Psalm 22:7-8 Isaiah 50:6	Matthew 26:67-68; 27:30 Mark 14:65
11	Messiah was to be mocked and taunted	Psalm 22:7-8	Matthew 27:39-43 Luke 23:11, 35
12	Messiah was to suffer with transgressors and pray for his enemies	Isaiah 53:12	Matthew 27:38 Mark 15:27-28 Luke 23:32-34
13	Messiah was to be given vinegar and gall	Psalm 69:21	Matthew 27:34 John 19:28-30
14	Others were to cast lots for Messiah's clothes	Psalm 22:18	Matthew 27:35 John 19:24
15	Messiah was to die by crucifixion	Psalm 22:14, 16, 17	Matthew 27:31 Mark 15:20, 25
16	Messiah's bones were not to be broken.	Exodus 12:46	John 19:31-36
17	Messiah's side would be pierced	Zechariah 12:10	John 19:34
18	Darkness would cover the land	Amos 8:9	Matthew 27:45
19	Messiah was to die as a sacrifice for sin	Isaiah 53:5, 6, 8, 10-12	John 1:29; 11:47-52 Acts 10:43; 13:38-39
20	Messiah would be buried in a rich man's grave	Isaiah 53:9	Matthew 27:57-60
21	Messiah was to be raised from the dead	Psalm 16:10	Acts 2:22-32 Matthew 28:1-10
22	Messiah is now at God's right hand	Psalm 110:1	Mark 16:19 Luke 24:50-51

Approximate year the above-mentioned books of the Bible were written:

Deuteronomy—1400 B.C.

Micah—700 B.C.

Amos—755 B.C.

Isaiah—Between 700 B.C. and 680 B.C.

Zechariah—Between 520 B.C. and 480 B.C.

Psalms—Between 1440 B.C. and 586 B.C.

Exodus—1450 B.C.

Matthew—A.D. 80

Mark—A.D. 64

Luke—A.D. 75

John—A.D. 95

Acts—A.D. 75

You Can Make a Difference by Taking the HomeTown Challenge

Young people, like you, often have a strong desire to make a difference for God but are unsure of what that means . . . and how to do it. What *can* you do when you want to reach out with Christ's love?

Youth for Christ has created three resource packets. Each packet contains practical suggestions of how you can make a difference in one of these areas:

Packet #1. "How to Start an Equal Access Club" —Do you know you have a legal right to meet for prayer or Bible study at your school?

Packet #2. "How to Share Jesus with a Friend" —Young people all over are discovering that they can lead a friend to Jesus when they know what to do and what to say.

Packet #3. "How to Hold a Training or Outreach Event" —You and your Christian friends can hold a special event for evangelism training and/or reaching out to others with the Good News of Jesus.

Call Youth for Christ at 1-800-729-DC94 to find out how you can sign up for one of these HomeTown Challenges and get information about youth evangelism training. Or write: Youth for Christ/USA, HomeTown Challenge, P.O. Box 228822, Denver, CO 80222

How Possessive Are You?

Possessive friends don't stay tight very long. People enjoy being around someone who's secure enough to provide the space needed for quality friendships. Girls, we especially find it easy to fall into the "possessiveness trap."

(Guys, since I don't think you struggle as much with this as girls, I've used only girls names here. If you DO have a problem in this area, simply change some of the girls' names to guys' names.)

What about YOU? Check your possessiveness factor by taking this quick quiz.

1. You and Jamie both have the same class before lunch and walk to the school cafeteria together. You've been friends only since September but have established a close relationship and enjoy eating lunch together.

Today Jamie asked Cindy (the new transfer student) if she'd like to join the two of you for lunch. You . . .

a. are excited about making a new friend.

b. talk with Cindy, but wish Jamie had asked you about including her first.

c. feel threatened, wondering if Cindy and Jamie will become better friends than *you* and Jamie.

2. Three weeks ago you made plans with Sarah to spend Saturday afternoon at the mall. Saturday morning she calls to inform you that her grandpar-

ents are in town, and she's doing things with her family all afternoon. You . . .

a. wonder if they're really in town, or if Sarah is just trying to get out of going to the mall with you.

b. stop by her house to make sure she really has company.

c. are disappointed but make plans to do the same thing the following weekend.

3. You always sit with Marissa in youth group. *This* week, however, she suggests you both sit with people you don't know very well, in an effort to get to know more of the other teens. You . . .

a. agree that you both need more friends and begin thinking about teens who possibly feel left out.

b. wonder what you did to make Marissa mad at you.

c. realize she's trying to tell you to "back off."

4. Once you've established a close friendship, you . . .

a. spend most of your time with her and don't really need anyone else.

b. enjoy your friend while still maintaining other special friendships.

c. get worried, angry, or pan-

icked if you don't hear from her or see her on a regular basis.

5. You've been friends with Dawn for two years. Lately, though, she's seemed distant and evasive. She's also missed church for three weeks in a row and is starting to hang around with kids at school who have a bad rep. You . . .

a. call her mom and make sure she knows what Dawn is doing.

b. share your concern with Dawn and remind her how much you value her friendship.

c. call her daily and tell her she's headed for trouble if she doesn't get her act together.

6. Your locker partner, Traci, is crying when you get to school. You ask her what's wrong, but she says she doesn't want to talk about it. You . . .

a. respond, "Fine! Be that way."

b. write her a note during class, find her at lunch, and catch up with her after school, begging her to tell you what's wrong.

c. call her after school and say, "Hope things are going bet-

212

ter for you. Just want to remind you that I care."

7. You agreed to meet Debbie at the winter hayride, but when you arrive she's talking with Josh. They invite you to sit with them on the wagon, but you decline because you're hoping Kenny will ask you to sit with *him*. Kenny, however, sits with Monica, and you end up next to some kids you don't know very well.

It's obvious Debbie and Josh are having fun together; they giggle the entire ride. Afterward, you . . .

a. tell Debbie, "I felt a little uncomfortable and left out . . . but I'm excited you and Josh got to sit together. Tell me every detail."

b. tell your other friends that Debbie was super-flirting with Josh and that you heard from your brother's cousin that he didn't make good grades and was suspended last year for something.

c. stick close to Debbie and interrupt whenever Josh starts to say something, so she won't forget *you're* her best friend.

8. Linzey asks you to attend the carnival with her. You can't ▼

help but notice how fast she's spending her money. You . . .

a. grab her purse and say, "Are you crazy? It's stupid to spend money on those flaky games. You *know* they're rigged! I'm hanging on to the rest of this *for* you."

b. make her think by laughing and saying, "Whatta ya gonna do when that's all gone? We just got here, Linz. Slow down so we can make the fun last longer."

c. simply think, *She deserves the rotten time she's gonna have when her money's all gone in thirty minutes. That's what she gets for spending it on dumb stuff.*

9. It's Friday afternoon, and you've invited Shelby to come over and watch TV, make popcorn, and spend the night. She says she'd like to but has to do homework this particular evening. You . . .

a. say, "OK, what about *this?* Bring your homework over, and I'll help you with it . . . or if your parents won't let you do *that,* let's try to make plans for *next* Friday."

b. respond, "Aw, Shelby, come on! You have the entire weekend to do homework. You never wanna have fun anymore. Please? We'll have loads of fun. You can do it, can't ya? Come on!"

c. say, "Well, if you hadn't gone to the mall with Sheri yesterday after school you could've finished all your homework. How come you'll do stuff with *her* but not with *me?*"

10. You've looked forward to your youth group's retreat for a long time. It's Saturday afternoon, and you want Lisa to ride the paddle boats with you. She's reading a book. This morning you tried to talk her into going hiking but she was playing volleyball with some other teens. You . . .

a. can't understand why she doesn't like you anymore.

b. are scared that you're losing a good friend.

c. try to understand that you both have different ideas about how to relax and have fun. Later, you ask her what *she'd* like to do.

Scoring

Calculate your score according to the chart below.

1. A=5, B=2, C=0
2. A=2, B=0, C=5
3. A=5, B=2, C=0
4. A=2, B=5, C=0
5. A=2, B=5, C=0
6. A=2, B=0, C=5
7. A=5, B=2, C=0
8. A=0, B=5, C=2
9. A=5, B=2, C=2
10. A=0, B=2, C=5

40–50 Gr-r-reat Friend!

Congrats! You're definitely a "people person." You enjoy being around others and feel secure enough to give your friends the healthy space they need. You don't smother them, and you probably enjoy trying to bring out the very best in them.

You're also good at reaching out, and you enjoy making new friends while maintaining close contact with others. *You're* the kind of friend *we'd* like to have! So take a pix of you and your best friend reading this book, and send it our way.

25–39 Hesitant Friend

You know you need to include others, but hesitate to do so. Why? Well, for starters, you're probably struggling with insecurity, jealousy, or fear. Can you talk with your parents or youth minister about developing a better self-image?

Your feelings are easily hurt, you develop bad attitudes quickly, and you tend to be pretty possessive with the few close friends you have. Learn to give them proper space (don't demand they always hang around you; let them enjoy other friendships) or you'll lose your friends pretty quickly.

Here's *our* challenge: Take a pix of you, a friend, and one of your parents all reading this book together. You need the input of an adult to develop some more positive friendship qualities. We'll hang your pix on our office bulletin board because we believe you're filled with tons of friendship potential!

0–24 Not a Friend

Wowsers. We need to go get a Coke and talk for a looooong time. Sad, but you haven't really learned how to be a good friend. You're extremely possessive with the "friends" you have, but we're wondering if you actually have any *true* friends at all.

It's easy for you to read between the lines and look for hidden motives that actually may not even exist. For instance when a friend has to cancel plans with you, don't im-

mediately assume she doesn't like you anymore. Strive to increase your trust level, since it's often hard for you to believe what your friends tell you.

You probably have a history of losing friends. You *want* close friendships, but when they begin to develop, you start doing the things mentioned above. That makes others back off.

Why do you do this? Probably because you're *afraid* of close relationships, or because you just haven't learned good friendship skills.

Pleeeeze talk with your parents or youth minister about helping you become the friend to others that you really want to be. Our suggestion: Take a pix of you and at least four other girls reading this book together, so we'll know you're *trying* to develop more friendships. We'll look forward to hearing your success story.

Tyndale's Got Great Guidance for the Issues in Your Life!